GW01216658

BELITHA
Information
LIBRARY

ECOLOGY
AND
CONSERVATION

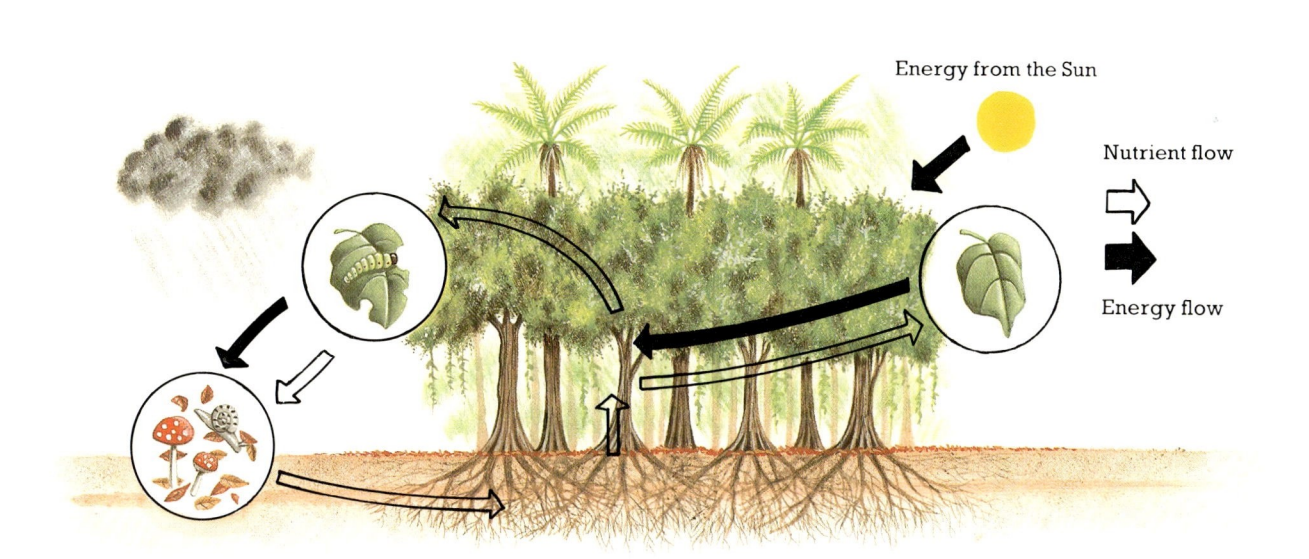

Energy from the Sun

Nutrient flow

Energy flow

STEVEN SEIDENBERG

 BELITHA PRESS

First published in Great Britain in 1990 by
Belitha Press Limited
31 Newington Green, London N16 9PU
Copyright © Belitha Press Limited and
Gareth Stevens, Inc. 1990
Illustrations/photographs copyright © in this
format by Belitha Press Limited and Gareth
Stevens, Inc. 1990
ISBN 1 85561 010 8
Typeset by Chambers Wallace, London
Printed in the UK for Imago Publishing
by MacLehose and Partners

British Library Cataloguing in Publication Data
CIP data for this book is available from the British
Library

Acknowledgements

Photographic credits:

Aspect Picture Library 23
Susan Griggs/McIntyre 51 top
Susan Griggs/Howarth 51 bottom
Robert Harding Picture Library 21 top
John Hillelson 14 bottom, 21 bottom, 28
Jimmy Holmes 49
Magnum 5, 11 top, 25, 38
Massey Ferguson 17 top
D. C. Money 32, 50
Marion and Tony Morrison 9 top, 14 top, 16 bottom,
   45
Natural Science Photos 11 middle & bottom, 12
   bottom, 37, 39, 48, 58, 59
Oxford Scientific Films 12 top, 35, 36, 43, 53
Panos Pictures 27, 42
Planet Earth 57
Frank Spooner 17 bottom, 30, 31
Telegraph Colour Library 4
   45
Thames Water Authority 33

Illustrated by: David Holmes and Eugene Fleury

Series editor: Neil Champion
Educational consultant: Dr Alistair Ross
Editorial consultant: Neil Morris
Designed by: Groom and Pickerill
Picture research and art editing: Ann Usborne

Contents

Words found in **bold** are explained
in the glossary on pages 60 and 61

1: ONLY ONE EARTH

The Living Planet

Earth is one of nine planets in the **solar system**. It is different from the other planets in that it can support life. This means that animals and plants can live on it. They can live because the Earth has the air they need to breathe, the **nutrients** they need to grow and a climate that is not too hot or too cold.

Life does not exist everywhere on Earth. There are some places, like hot deserts, frozen wastes or deep under ground, where the conditions are not right.

The **zone** in which plants and animals can live is called the **biosphere**. This is made up of three natural regions: the air, the ocean and the land. These three regions **interact** with each other to produce the life-supporting conditions that animals and plants need.

The Water Cycle

The water cycle is a good example of the interaction between the three life zones. The sun heats up the water in the seas and oceans of the

The biosphere

The atmosphere

The lithosphere   **The hydrosphere**

▲ The biosphere is made of three parts. The air (or atmosphere), the land (or lithosphere) and the water (or hydrosphere). The word 'biosphere' comes from the ancient Greek word 'bio' which means 'life'. Earth is the only planet in our solar system with a biosphere. It is a living planet.

When seen from outer space ▶ the blue oceans, the brown land, and the white clouds of our planet Earth are clear.

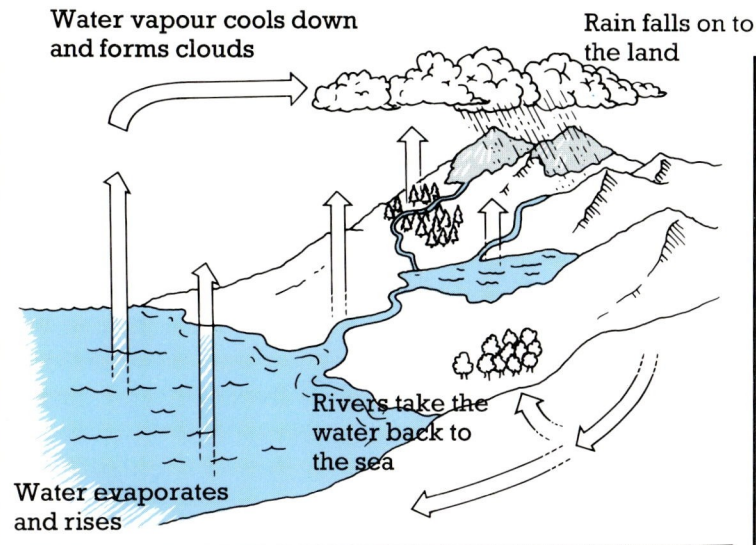

Water vapour cools down and forms clouds

Rain falls on to the land

Rivers take the water back to the sea

Water evaporates and rises

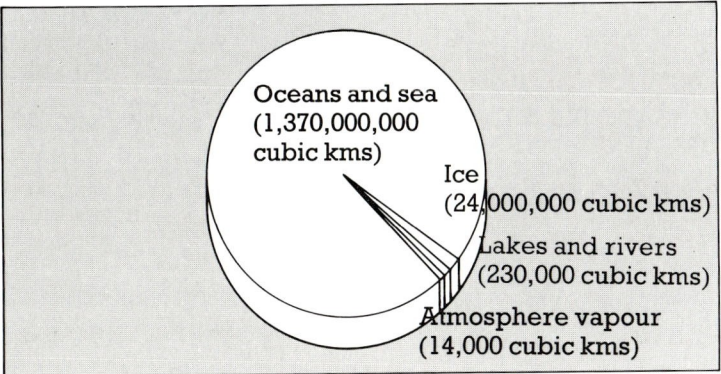

Oceans and sea
(1,370,000,000 cubic kms)

Ice
(24,000,000 cubic kms)

Lakes and rivers
(230,000 cubic kms)

Atmosphere vapour
(14,000 cubic kms)

◀ **The Water Cycle.** Water is heated by the Sun and evaporates. It rises and cools in the air, forming clouds, especially over mountains. It eventually falls back to Earth in the form of rain. Rain is gathered in streams and rivers and taken back to the sea.

hydrosphere. This causes some water to **evaporate** and rise into the **atmosphere**. As the water vapour rises, it cools down and forms clouds. The water in the clouds can be blown for hundreds or even thousands of miles before it eventually falls to the Earth again as salt-free rain or snow. Here it can be used by plants and animals as drinking water, before it begins its journey back to the sea in the form of streams and rivers. Then the cycle begins again. It is quite amazing to think that about two thirds of our planet is covered by water.

People are Threats

Human activities can threaten this balance. Cutting down too many trees, polluting the air or the water, or by allowing deserts to get bigger are all ways in which people disrupt the **environment**. If too much damage is done, the Earth will be in danger. It could stop being a living planet.

▲ Threats to the environment from pollution created by people have increased tremendously in the 20th century. Here we see the effects on a beach of an oil spill from a supertanker. Birds and fishes are particularly vulnerable.

The Web of Life

In our ocean food chain tiny plankton are eaten by krill. Small fish eat the krill and are themselves eaten by larger fish. Some fish are eaten by seals, which then are eaten by people. ▼

Life on Earth is abundant. There are millions of different kinds of plants and animals. Each **species** of plant or animal has something special that sets it apart from all others.

Chemicals of Life

Although each species is different, they all have one thing in common. They are made of the same building blocks of life. These are four **chemicals**: carbon, nitrogen, oxygen and hydrogen. These chemicals are also found in the environment, in the air, water and in the land. Animals cannot get them easily from these places but plants can. They take in the nutrients through their roots. Green plants, through a process called **photo-synthesis**, also change sunlight into food. Plants are then eaten by some animals. These animals are in turn eaten by other animals. This is how energy and the chemical building blocks are transferred from the soil, the air and sunlight through plants to animals, including human beings.

A Food Chain (I)

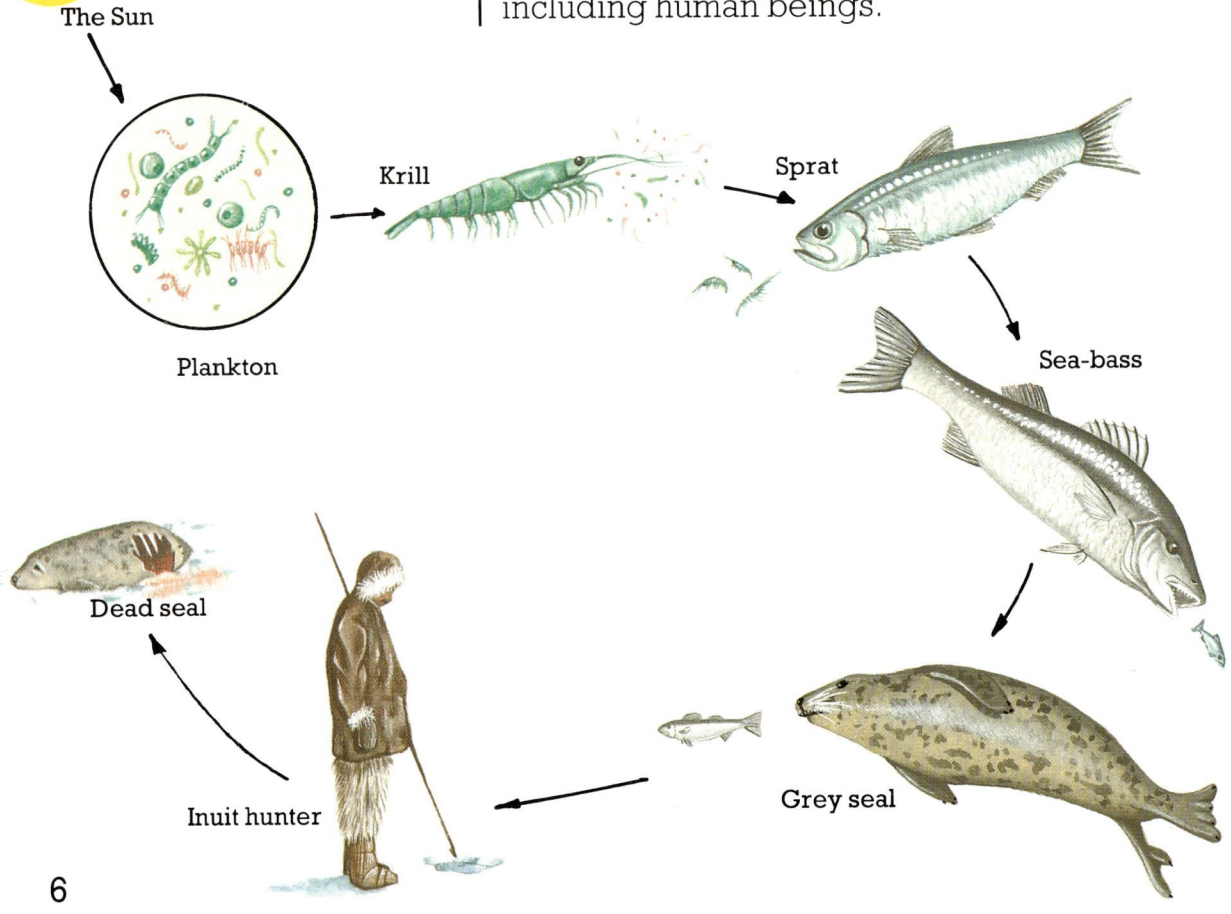

The Sun

Plankton

Krill

Sprat

Sea-bass

Dead seal

Inuit hunter

Grey seal

6

The Food Chain

Animals cannot live without plants. They are linked by this web of life, called a food chain. Each living thing is a food for another living thing. There are many different food chains. In the forest there might be a very short one: plant-insect-shrew-owl. In the African savannah a typical food chain would be grass-zebra-lion. Food chains in the sea are longer than those on land but they work the same way. A typical one might be: plankton-krill-small fish – **predatory** fish-gull-seal. These are simple food chains.

Food chains are very fragile and can be easily broken. Removing just one link can endanger the whole chain. For example, farmers use **pesticides** to kill insects that eat their crops. Once the insects have gone, shrews which eat them may starve and die out. Owls which eat shrews will then be short of food and they might die. This is just one example which shows just how delicate the web of life is.

In a forest food chain insects eat tree leaves. Small birds, like sparrows, eat the insects and are, in turn, eaten by carnivorous birds like this hawk. When the hawk dies insects like this sexton beetle help return its remains to the soil, where they form important nutrients for the growing tree. ▼

A Food Chain (II)

The Sun

Caterpillar

Sparrow

Sparrow hawk

Tree

Sexton beetle

Pollution

Acid rain damages forests. The top branch in the inset is of a healthy pine tree. The bottom branch shows the effects of acid rain. ▼

Pollution is one of the greatest threats to the environment. It can affect all parts of the biosphere. The atmosphere (air), lithosphere (land) and hydrosphere (water) all suffer from pollution.

Pollution is generally not a natural thing. People are the cause of pollution. Humans pollute the air with smoke and gases, the rivers, lakes and seas with sewage and harmful chemicals. The land is polluted with **fertilizers** and pesticides. Very often its effects are easy to see. Oil spilt in the sea can be seen for miles around. Animals affected by it, like birds or fish, can be seen dead on the beaches or floating in the water.

Industry

Most pollution comes from countries with big industries. Factories and cars give off fumes that contain poisonous chemicals. Sulphur

Healthy pine tree branch

The effects of acid rain

Tree damaged by acid rain

dioxide is one of these. When it mixes with water in the air it makes a weak **acid**. Acid rain can damage trees and buildings. In the air, this acid can be carried thousands of kilometres, affecting the environment of people in other countries.

Pollution is hard to control and some of its effects are long lasting and hard to put right. The situation is very complicated. Many things that cause pollution are of benefit to people: cars that get us around, factories that make important products and provide jobs, power stations that produce electricity, fertilizers that increase a farmer's crop yield.

Preventing Pollution

It is therefore not easy to prevent pollution happening. It is important that the problems are identified and the worst of them are tackled. Governments need to pass laws on the more dangerous forms of pollution. Scientists and engineers must find ways to clean up the environment and still have industries producing things.

▲ A thick haze of smog hangs in the air over Mexico City. This smoky fog is dangerous to breathe and it damages the environment. The pollution of the air is one of the biggest problems facing us today.

Oil and chemicals in the water and garbage on this beach are ruining this environment. Few things can live amongst such pollution. ▼

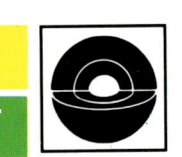

2: PLANET EARTH

The Earth's Crust

Rivers carry tiny pieces of rock down to the seas and oceans. ▶

The lithosphere is the surface land of the planet Earth. It does not include the hot **magma** and molten rock that make up the core of the Earth. Soil, which is the top layer of the planet, is part of the Earth's crust. It is thinner than the atmosphere or the hydrosphere but most of the different species of animals and plants live on or in it.

Soil is made up of two different kinds of things: tiny pieces of broken-up rock and rotting **organic** material. These trap air and water and provide the ideal conditions for most plants to grow.

Rock, water and air are the **inorganic** parts of the soil. Tiny pieces of rock make up more than half the soil. Together with water and air they provide the nutrients for the **micro-organisms** that live in the soil. These micro-organisms and the soil together combine to

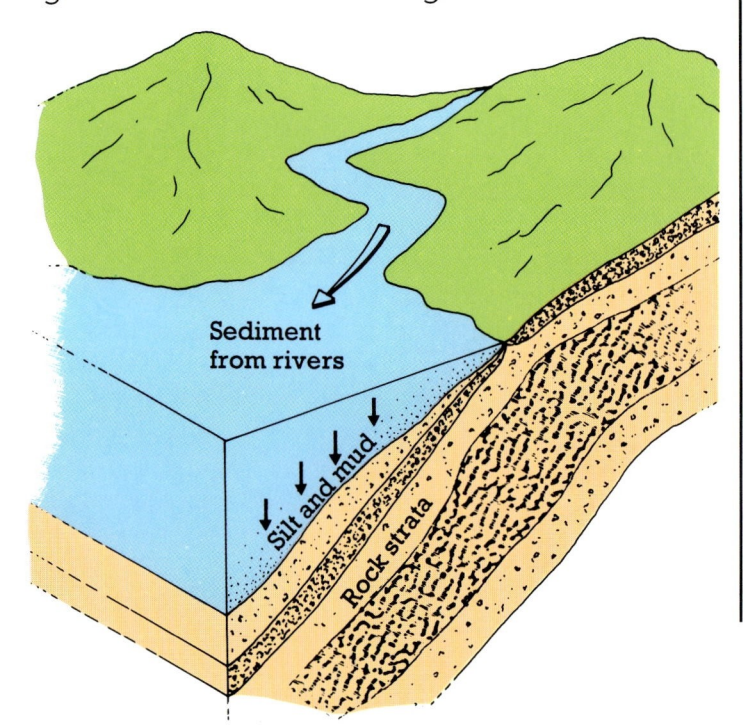

Sediment from rivers

Silt and mud

Rock strata

make the environment for plants. Dead organic material – called **humus** – is the last vital ingredient for healthy soil. This decaying plant material and the micro-organisms, living and dead make the soil rich. They help make it **fertile** so other plants can live.

Making Soil

It takes many years for natural forces to make soil. This is because the **weathering** process which makes soil is very slow. Wind and water take a long time to wear down rocks into the tiny particles which make up the soil. To make just one centimetre (less than half an inch) of new soil from rocks may take 1000 years. Unfortunately the destruction of soil by **erosion** is much faster. Each year 75 billion tonnes of soil are lost through erosion. Most of this erosion is caused by people. They do not take care of the land. Then the wind comes and blows it away or rains come and wash it away.

Unfortunately, although people are the cause of most of the soil destruction, they cannot make new soil. Only nature's weathering process can turn rock into soil. People cannot. Because people cannot make soil it is especially important for them to stop doing things which cause erosion.

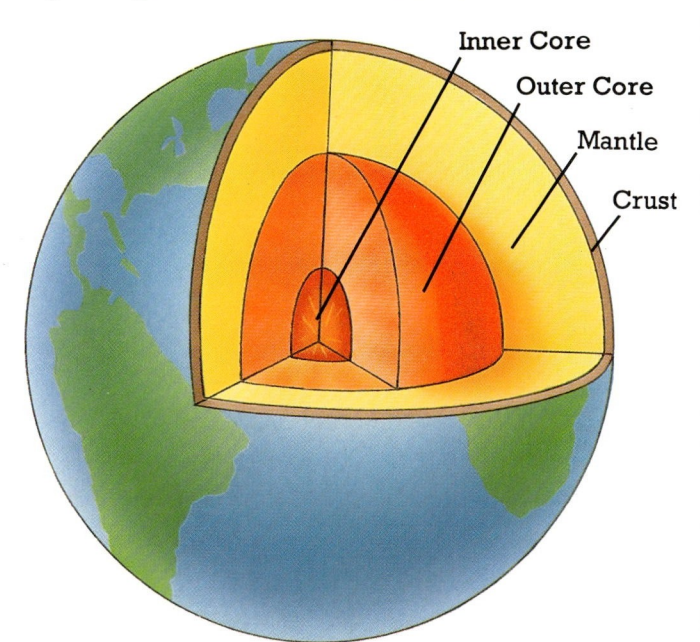

▲ The lithosphere has many different kinds of environments. The frozen wastes of Antarctica, rolling farmland, and the tropical rainforest are just three of the many different kinds of environments found on the Earth's surface.

◄ A cross-section through the Earth.

Animals

Healthy crops grow in the rich soil of the American Midwest (left). The dry, thin soils of the African Sahel (right) are poor for farming. ▶

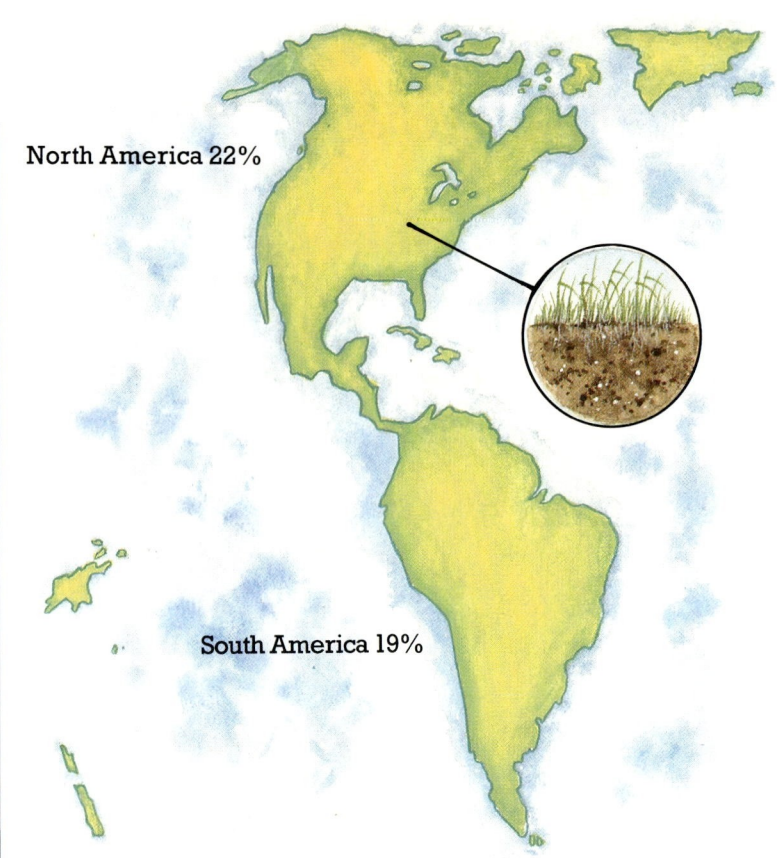

North America 22%

South America 19%

▲ This earthworm (above) and these wood ants (below) are just some of the animals whose activities help make the soil fertile. They do this by constantly breaking up debris on the forest floor.

Healthy soil is full of life. It contains millions of tiny animals and billions of micro-organisms. One **hectare** of good soil may contain 300 million tiny animals – insects, worms, millipedes, and countless other kinds of creatures. The same soil will contain many times more micro-organisms. There may be 100 million specimens of just one kind of **bacterium** in a spoonful of soil. And that spoonful of soil will have not just one but many different types of bacteria and other **microbes** in it. That same spoonful may also be home to 100,000 yeast cells and 50,000 bits of fungus. Good soil is teeming with life.

These tiny creatures and micro-organisms are very important for life on this planet. They do many things. Worms are a good example. By eating the soil the worms help break down the rock particles into even smaller pieces. Their tunnels are important because they help rainwater soak into the soil. The tunnels also serve as passages that help get air into the soil. Some microbes are important because they help trap gases, like nitrogen, in the soil. Once trapped, the nitrogen, can then be used

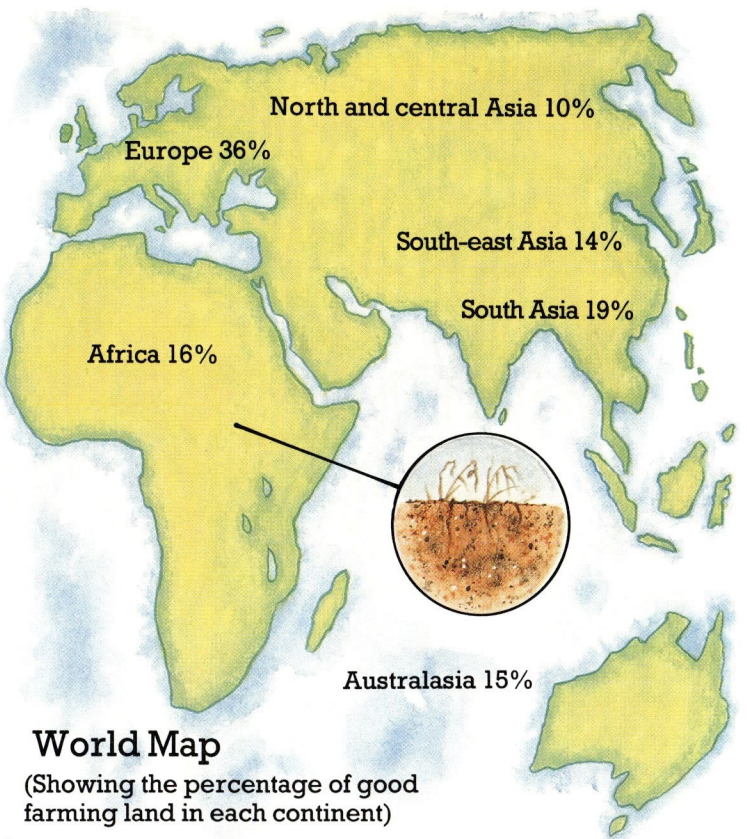

North and central Asia 10%

Europe 36%

South-east Asia 14%

South Asia 19%

Africa 16%

Australasia 15%

World Map
(Showing the percentage of good farming land in each continent)

by plants. Microbes are the first link in the food chain. Without them there would be no other plants or animals on Earth.

Different Soils

Not all soil is the same. The type of parent rock, the type and amount of organic and inorganic materials, even the weather can affect the soil. Only a small percentage of the Earth's soil has a favourable mix of these things. Not all surface land can be used for agriculture. In fact, most land is *not* suited for growing crops. Only 11 per cent of the Earth's land is good for farming. The other 89 per cent is either too dry, cold, wet, shallow or poor in nutrients.

Good farm land (arable land) is not distributed evenly around the world. Some countries have more good land than others. Europe is the continent with the highest percentage of arable land. Over one-third of the land can be used to grow crops. North and central Asia has the lowest percentage of arable land. There only 10 per cent of the land is usable. Good land everywhere is disappearing through erosion.

Facts & Feats

● There are more living organisms in one handful of good soil than there are on the entire planet Jupiter, the largest planet in our solar system.

● The deepest soils found in the world are the **loess** soils of north China and the Mississippi Valley in the United States. These soils can be more than 30 metres (100 feet) thick. They are full of organic matter and are especially fertile. Norway is a country with very thin soil. On average, the Norwegian soil is little more than 10 cms (4 ins) deep.

● There are 1.5 billion hectares (4 billion acres) of farm land in the world. Each year more than 2 million hectares (5 million acres) are completely ruined by erosion.

● Naturally rich soil gives much better harvests than poor soil. One acre of naturally rich soil in Iowa or East Anglia will yield as much in one year as 4 hectares (10 acres) of naturally poor soil in Bolivia or Zambia.

● The United Kingdom and Japan have the highest cereal crop yields per hectare in the world. They produce 7 times as much cereal per hectare of farmland than Nigeria. They also use 60 times as much fertilizer and other agricultural chemicals than Nigeria.

● Not all arable land is currently being used for farming. Europe has the highest percentage of arable land actually under plough. Eighty-one per cent of the arable land in Europe is being farmed. Latin America is the continent with the most under-used land resources. Only 19 per cent of the arable land in Latin America is being used.

Losing Ground

▲ Clearing these hillside slopes for farmland has caused serious erosion. The bare slopes of these Andean hills were left unprotected from the rains. Most of the soil has been washed away. Now there is almost none left.

Some of the worst erosion in history happened in the American west in the 1930s. Bad farming methods left the soil unprotected. Fierce winds blew it away. This dust storm, like a cloud of black smoke, shows how it was blown away. (See also page 40). ▶

Although we cannot live without healthy soil we are destroying over 3,000 tonnes of it every second. This is a terrible waste of a precious **resource**. Worse, it is not a resource we can replace. Unlike polluted air or water which can be cleaned, once the soil is destroyed it is gone for ever.

Erosion

Soil is destroyed in many different ways. One of these, erosion, is a major problem. Wind and water are the chief agents of erosion. Wind can blow away and water can wash away vast quantities of soil. Most of the soil carried by the wind falls on the ocean. The soil washed away by rain first runs into rivers. These rivers then carry it to the ocean. Once in the ocean the soil is lost for ever.

When erosion is natural it happens slowly. But this natural process can be speeded up by bad agricultural practices. This is because soil is fragile. It needs a protective cover of plants to keep it from being blown or washed away. The leaves of plants act as umbrellas protecting the soil. They protect it from the force of the wind and the rain. The roots of plants help bind the soil together. They also help channel the rainwater safely away.

Water erosion

Wind erosion

Over-grazing

Over-grazing is the main cause of **desertification**. Animals, such as sheep, goats, horses, llamas and camels, eat the ground vegetation and expose soil to the eroding effects of wind and rain.

There are other agricultural practices which destroy soil. **Irrigation** can be a useful way of bringing water to dry fields. Good irrigation systems bring the right amount of water to the plants. Good systems also take any excess water safely away. Without proper **drainage**, an irrigated field may become too wet or waterlogged. When this happens, plants have difficulty in surviving. Waterlogging can also break down the structure of the soil. Another problem with bad irrigation systems is that they can cause **salinization**. Irrigation water can carry damaging salts and leave them on the soil surface. These salts are harmful to plants and can kill them.

▲ Wind and water are the two biggest causes of erosion. Wind (right) can blow away all the soil and carve the bare rock which remains into fantastic shapes. Water can wash away the soil, carving deep gulleys.

Did You Know?

Bad farming practices destroy the soil's vegetation cover. When the soil is left bare after harvest it is particularly easy for it to be blown or washed away. Crops sown in rows such as soybeans and maize (corn) are especially bad because they leave so much soil unprotected.

Saving the Soil

These terraces in Peru show how good farming methods can protect the soil on hillsides. Terraces slow rainwater down. Slowing the rainwater as it goes downhill is an important way of stopping water erosion. ▼

Just as there are many causes of erosion, so too are there many solutions. These solutions all come down to a single rule: good management of agricultural lands. Getting farmers to follow good farming practices is the fastest way to stop erosion.

Stopping Erosion

One of the most important ways of stopping erosion is to combat the effects of wind and water, which carry the soil away. We cannot stop the wind from blowing nor can we stop the rain from falling. But we can slow them down. When they lose their power they do not threaten the land so much. It is not a gentle breeze that carries clouds of dust and soil away. It is fierce winds that do this. Planting trees and hedgerows as **windbreaks** around fields does much to slow the destructive power of the wind.

The action of rainwater on soil is especially severe on hillsides. Unless special care is taken, rainwater builds up speed as it runs down the hill. The faster the water goes the

Did You Know?

There are several different things that farmers can do to stop erosion on cropland. Some – like **terracing** and **fallowing** – have been known for a long time. Others, like "**no-till ploughing**" are new solutions to the erosion problem.

◀ This American farmer is using the new technique of 'no-till' ploughing to plant his crops. This plough does not cut deep furrows in the land. It drills the seeds into the ground. This method of farming will help prevent wind erosion and dust storms, because it does not expose the soil by breaking its surface and turning it over.

These windbreaks have been built to stop precious soil being blown away. Inside the area penned in by the breaks, small saplings and grass are growing. The roots of these plants will also help hold the scarce soil in position and give other plants a chance to grow. ▼

more soil it carries away. The flow of rain-water can be slowed by building terraces and by **contour ploughing**. Terraces are cut into the hillside. This holds back the water. So, too, does ploughing furrows at an angle to the direction of the water-flow.

New Ploughing Methods

A new method of ploughing that helps protect cropland from erosion, is now being tried out. This new method, called "no-till ploughing", replaces the old method of leaving the ground bare for several months each year. In no-till ploughing the soil is never laid bare. Cut stalks from last year's crop are left in the fields. New seeds are sown by scratching a very shallow furrow or even with no furrow at all. By not turning the old plant remains into the soil it is never left bare and at the mercy of the wind and rain.

When proper care is taken in the design of irrigation systems, the problems of salinization and waterlogging can be overcome. Laying drains and the careful control of the water-flow can keep harmful salts away.

3: THE BREATHING PLANET

The Air

The Earth is surrounded by a huge bubble, or envelope, of gases. These gases are the air we breathe. We call the bubble the atmosphere. Although we cannot see, touch or usually smell the atmosphere, it is very important. All living things – animals and plants – need air to breathe. The atmosphere is important for other reasons as well. In the daytime, it acts as a screen which blocks out harmful **radiation** from the Sun. At night, it acts as a blanket which helps keep the Earth warm. The atmosphere also acts as a protective shield which causes most **meteorites** to burn up harmlessly before they reach the ground. Without its atmosphere, the Earth would be a dead planet. It would be pitted and pock-marked by meteorite craters. It would be deadly cold at night and too hot in the day.

Gas Cycles

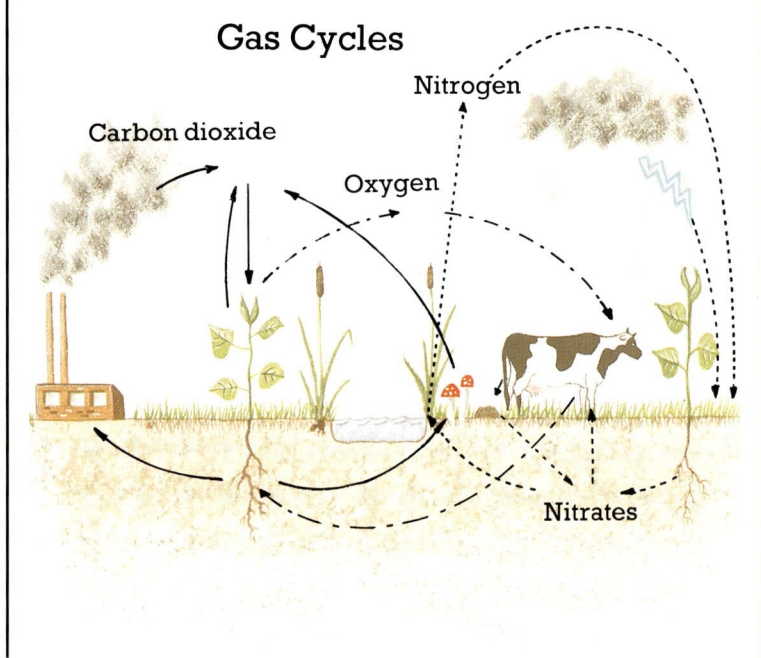

Carbon Dioxide (CO_2), Oxygen (O) and Nitrogen (N) are constantly recycled by the interaction of animals, plants, soil, sunlight and the atmosphere. ▶

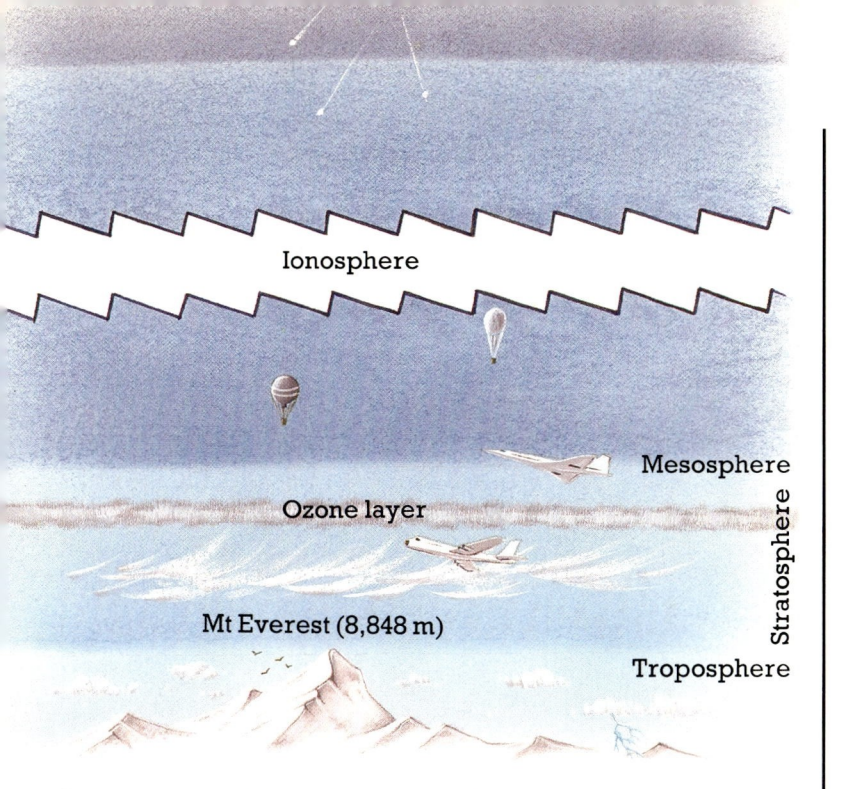

Ionosphere

Mesosphere

Ozone layer

Stratosphere

Mt Everest (8,848 m)

Troposphere

Gases of the Atmosphere

The atmospheric envelope contains many gases. Only three of them exist in large quantities. Nitrogen, oxygen and argon make up 99.9 per cent of the total **mass** of the atmosphere. There are tiny amounts of other gases – neon, helium, krypton, and xenon. Smoke, dust, water vapour and even some microbes also float in it. Together, all these things equal less than 0.1 per cent of the atmospheric mass.

The gases are not spread evenly. They are most dense close to the ground. Above 500 kms (300 miles) they hardly exist at all. One-half of the atmosphere's mass exists in the 5,500 metres (18,000 feet) closest to the ground. Ninety per cent of its mass is in the lowest 15 kms (9 miles). The remaining 10 per cent is spread thinly in the 1,000 kms (670 miles) of the upper atmosphere.

The atmosphere is divided into layers. The layer closest to the Earth's surface is called the troposphere. It is this layer which contains 90 per cent of the mass of the atmospheric gases. It is in the troposphere's great mass of moving air that the Earth's weather is found. The other layers of the atmosphere are the stratosphere, the mesosphere and the thermosphere.

◄ The main divisions of the atmosphere are the troposphere (up to 15 kms above the Earth's surface), the stratosphere (15 to 50 kms), and the mesosphere (50 to 80 kms). Most clouds are less than 5 kms above the Earth's surface. Jet planes fly at about 10 kms up. The ozone layer is around 20-25 kms up and the trails of meteors can be seen when they enter the atmosphere about 50 kms up.

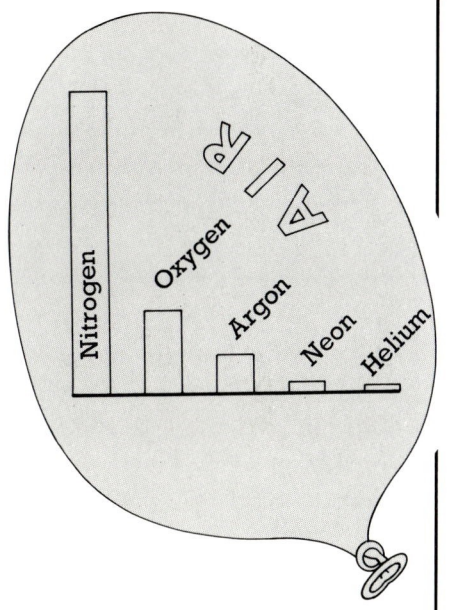

Nitrogen Oxygen Argon Neon Helium

▲ The air is made up of many gases. Nitrogen and oxygen are the most important.

The Human Cost

Facts & Feats

● In 1952 about 4,000 people died in London because of polluted air which caused 'killer fog'. Since then, laws have been passed to keep pollutants out of the London air.

● Each year, Europe produces 40 million tonnes of sulphur dioxide (SO_2) which passes into the air. It is created mainly by industrial activity. Only a small percentage is produced from natural sources (swamp gas, volcanoes and rotting vegetation).

● Nearly half of southern Norway's freshwater fish population is extinct. Air pollution resulting in acid rain has killed them. More than 18,000 lakes in Norway (22 per cent of Norway's lakes) are acidified.

● Over half the trees in the Black Forest of West Germany have been damaged by acid rain.

The Acid Rain Cycle. Pollution from factories, power stations and cars is released into the atmosphere. It mixes with water vapour in clouds to make an acid which can be carried for hundreds of miles before falling as acid rain and snow. ▶

Air is colourless, odourless and tasteless. We can only see it or smell it when it becomes polluted. Pollution occurs when waste materials get into the air. Most wastes come from human activities. The chief sources of these wastes are burning **fossil fuels**, industrial processes and burning solid wastes. Natural **pollutants** such as dust, pollen and soil particles do not cause environmental problems. Artificial pollutants do. They cause health problems in people and harm other living things. Plants and animals are harmed by air pollution. Air pollution can also harm buildings and fabrics. Most important of all, air pollution can harm the atmosphere itself.

Pollutants

There are two different forms that pollutants may take. They can be either gases which do not belong in the atmosphere or they can be tiny bits of airborne liquid or solid materials (called particulates). Soot and dust are two of the most common particulates in the atmosphere.

The Acid Rain Cycle

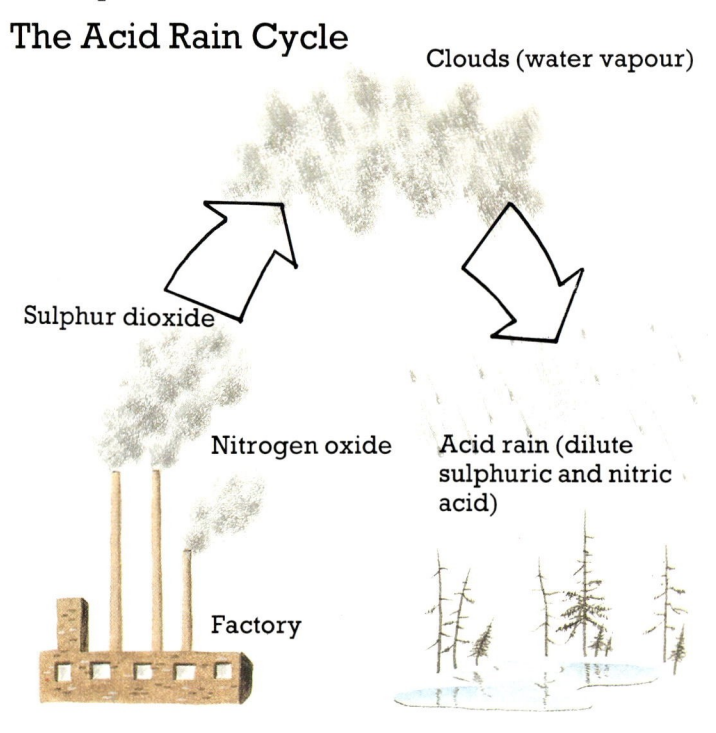

Clouds (water vapour)

Sulphur dioxide

Nitrogen oxide

Acid rain (dilute sulphuric and nitric acid)

Factory

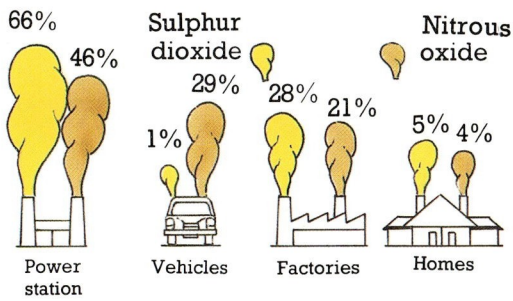

66% 46%	Sulphur dioxide 29%	28% 21%	Nitrous oxide 5% 4%
1%			
Power station	Vehicles	Factories	Homes

◀ The air pollution in Athens, Greece, is some of the worst in the world. Greek temples which are thousands of years old are now falling down because the air pollution is eating away at the stone.

In Japan the air pollution is so bad that many people wear masks to help keep it out. In Tokyo, the air is so bad that there are machines on street corners, like telephone boxes, where people can buy a breath of clean oxygen. ▼

Fossil Fuels

Burning fossil fuels – coal, oil, gas – is a major source of pollutants in the air. **Combustion** releases harmful gases such as sulphur dioxide (SO_2) and nitrous oxides (NO_x) into the air. Burning fuels also releases other gases and particulate matter such as soot into the air.

Fossil fuels are burned for many reasons. They are used to provide energy to run automobiles and factories, to heat our homes and to provide electricity. Fossil fuels are very useful. Pollutants released by their burning are not. These pollutants cause **acid rain**, one of the most harmful kinds of air pollution.

Acid rain occurs when pollutants such as SO_2 and NO_x combine with moisture in the air. Together they make clouds of acid. These clouds may carry the acids for several days and more than 1000 kms (620 miles) before they fall to Earth again as acid rain. This acid can be very harmful. As it builds up, it kills plants. Acid rainwater soaks into the soil and runs off into rivers and lakes. Acid in lakes and rivers can kill fish and other aquatic life. Acid eats away at buildings and monuments.

Polluted Poland

Poland is one of the most polluted countries in the world. Coal burned there is of very low quality and releases sulphur dioxide into the air. This produces acid rain. The acid rain has been known to eat into the metal railway tracks!

Polluting the Air

The Greenhouse Effect.
Pollution releases excessive amounts of carbon dioxide into the atmosphere. Just like a real greenhouse, the carbon dioxide acts as a barrier which lets the Sun's heat in but does not let it escape. This causes the general climatic conditions to get warmer. ▼

The atmosphere is a vast chemical cauldron. In it, naturally-occurring gases mix with the pollutants we put there. This mixing creates new and deadly products. Acid rain is just one of them.

Carbon Dioxide

Burning fossil fuels releases several gases. We have already seen how the sulphur dioxide and the nitrous oxides released this way form acid rain. Burning fossil fuels releases another gas as well. This is carbon dioxide (CO_2). Some CO_2 exists naturally in the atmosphere. It is an important and necessary gas. Plants breathe in CO_2 in their respiration cycle. But too much CO_2 in the atmosphere can create problems. It can act as a temperature barrier. This barrier acts like a greenhouse – it lets the sun's heat in, but it does not let it escape. This is worrying because it can make the whole Earth heat up. This would change the world climate and disrupt rainfall patterns. If the Earth gets just 3 degrees centigrade (5 degrees Fahrenheit) warmer whole eco-systems would be altered or destroyed.

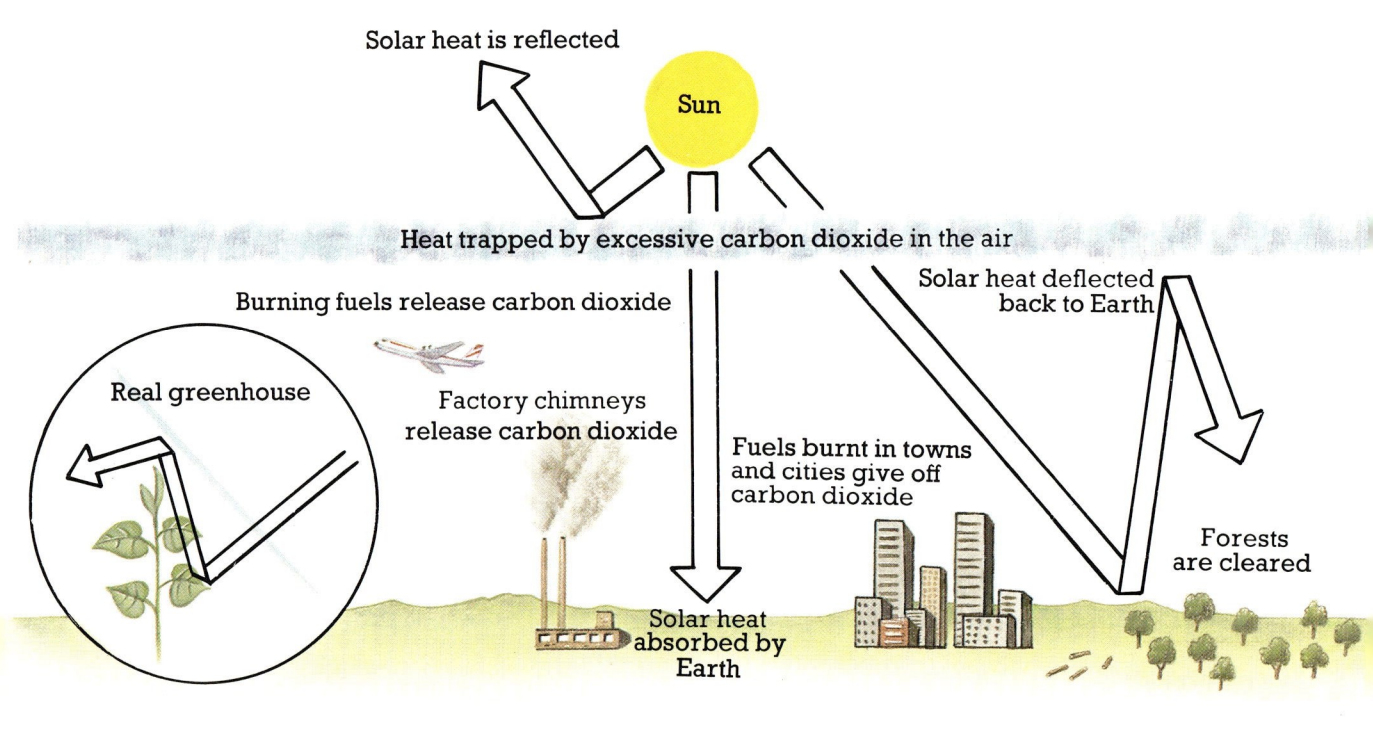

Solar heat is reflected

Sun

Heat trapped by excessive carbon dioxide in the air

Burning fuels release carbon dioxide

Solar heat deflected back to Earth

Real greenhouse

Factory chimneys release carbon dioxide

Fuels burnt in towns and cities give off carbon dioxide

Forests are cleared

Solar heat absorbed by Earth

◄ Los Angeles is the smoggiest city in the USA. It is ringed by mountains. When the weather conditions are right, smog can be trapped over the city for several days. Here the smog is so thick that it has turned the sky brown and totally blocked out the surrounding mountains.

◄ CFCs (chlorofluorocarbons) from some aerosol sprays, refrigerants and fast food packaging threaten the ozone layer. This chemical compound, once released into the atmosphere, can destroy the protective ozone.

Smog

Pollution threatens the atmosphere in another way as well. *Smog* (*smoky fog*) is made up of several different pollutants. One of them is ozone (O_3), a special form of oxygen. Ozone is unpleasant at ground level but it is very important in the atmosphere. Ozone forms a floating band about 50 kms (30 miles) above the Earth's surface. This ozone band is essential for life on Earth. The ozone layer acts as a shield. It absorbs harmful ultraviolet radiation from the sun and stops too much of this radiation from reaching the Earth. This is very important because too much ultraviolet radiation can cause cancer in humans. It can also cause damage to plants and animals.

The Ozone

Man-made chemicals can attack the ozone layer. One group of chemicals – the chlorofluorocarbons (CFCs) – is particularly harmful. We use these chemicals for many things. CFCs are used in refrigerators as a cooling agent. They are the gas frequently used in aerosol spray cans. They are also used to make the foam plastic packages that some hamburgers come in. When CFCs are released into the atmosphere they react with the ozone and destroy it.

Cleaning the Air

Air does not have to be polluted. We can stop atmospheric pollution. There are several steps which can be taken. Because power stations are the major cause of acid rain, it is important that we clean them up. Some steps are simple to take. Burning only high-quality coal and oil is a first step already taken by many industrial countries. This coal is more expensive than low-quality coal, but it is better for the environment. **Scrubbers** and filters attached to power station chimneys trap harmful pollutants before they are released into the atmosphere.

Designing new Engines

It is possible to control the emissions from vehicles in the same way. New engines have been designed which reduce the amount of pollutants released into the atmosphere. These 'lean-burn' engines are more efficient and make fewer pollutants than other engines. Engines designed to run on lead-free petrol cut down on the amount of lead released into the environment. Cars, trucks and buses can be fitted with their own scrubbers, called 'catalytic converters'. Attached to the

Hydro-electric Dam

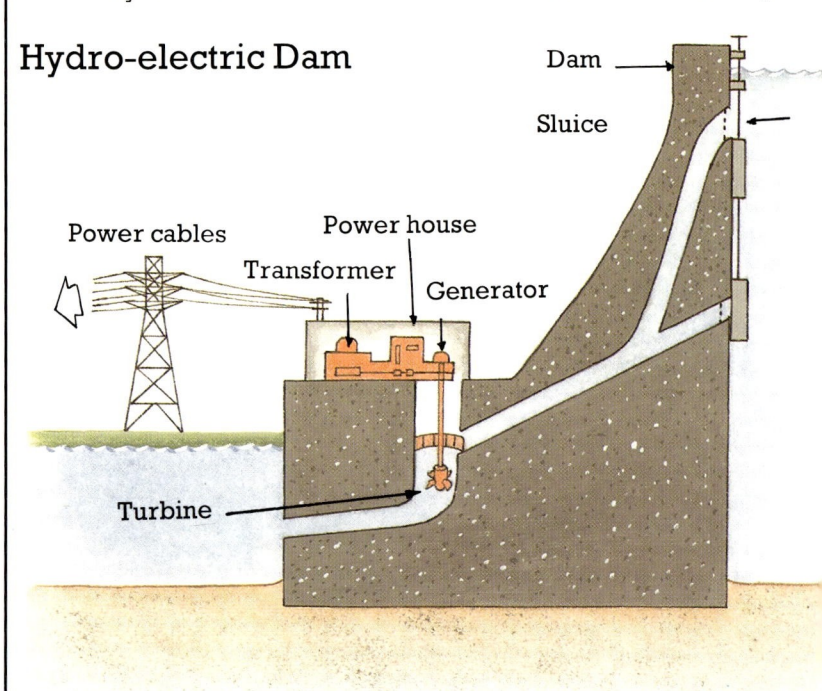

Hydro-electric power stations use water-power to make electricity. Water from behind the dam (right) is let out to turn a turbine which makes electricity. This is a clean way of making energy which does not cause pollution. ▶

exhaust pipes of vehicles these devices act like the scrubbers on power station chimneys.

It is not as easy to control the CFCs. No cheap alternative to them has yet been found. It is possible, however, to limit their use. Restricting CFCs to essential uses – such as refrigeration – and stopping their use for such things as disposable packaging, is an important step to take. Some countries have already passed laws restricting the use of CFC's. We can all help by refusing to buy aerosols that use CFCs or fast-foods that are packed in the CFC foam cartons.

The Cure

Curing the effects of air pollution is very expensive. Scrubbers and emission controls cost a lot to install and to operate. Alternatives to CFCs and other useful chemicals are also expensive. Preventing pollutants from entering the atmosphere in the first place can be much cheaper in the long run. Using less power and driving our cars less often are just two steps that we can each take to stop atmospheric pollution.

▲ Using clean sources of energy are one way to help reduce the levels of pollution. These wind pumps in California, USA, use the power of the wind as their source of energy.

Did You Know?

Governments and companies have invested in new sources of energy which do not rely on fossil fuels. Wind power now provides electricity for the national grid in California. Wave power and tidal power are providing electricity in several locations around the world. Experiments with solar power are attempting to harness this clean source of energy. These non-polluting sources of energy could be very important in the future.

4: A Watery World

A Blue Planet

Two-thirds of the Earth's surface is water. The Pacific is the largest ocean. ▶

Facts & Feats

● The longest river is the Nile (6,670 kms or 4,445 miles).

● The river draining the largest area is the Amazon. Its basin area is over 7 million sq. kms (nearly 3 million sq. miles).

● The Amazon is also the river which discharges the greatest amount of water into the sea. Over 180,000 cubic metres (6 million cubic feet) empty into the ocean from it every second.

● Lake Superior of the North American Great Lakes is the world's largest fresh water lake. Its total area is over 82,000 sq. kms (almost 32,000 sq. miles).

● Lake Baikal in the USSR is the world's deepest lake. It is 1,741 metres (5,712 feet) at its deepest point.

● Tremendous volumes of water are involved in the hydrological cycle. In a single year 333,500 cubic kilometres (80,000 cubic miles) of seawater are drawn off through evaporation to fall back to earth as rain. About one-third of this water falls on land. The rest falls on the ocean where it can evaporate again.

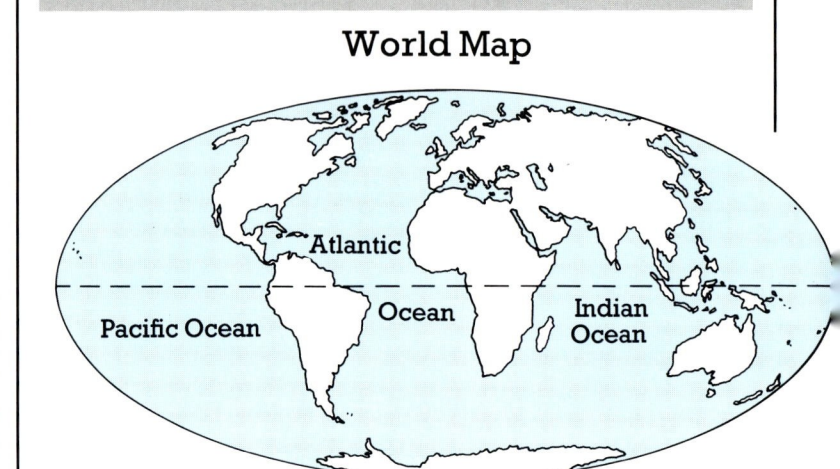

World Map

Pacific Ocean — Atlantic — Ocean — Indian Ocean

The Earth appears to be a blue planet when seen from outer space. This is because more than two-thirds of the Earth's surface is water. We call this water the **hydrosphere**.

Water is Precious

Water is necessary for life. Neither plants nor animals can live without it. It has special characteristics which make it rare in the solar system. Water can only exist in a narrow range of temperatures: if too hot, it changes into a gas; too cold and it changes to ice.

The Water Cycle

Water moves in a continuous cycle through the hydrosphere, the lithosphere and the atmosphere. In the water (or hydrological) cycle, heat causes water to evaporate from the surface of the seas, rivers and lakes. Water vapour is also given off through the **transpiration** of plants. The water vapour from evaporation and from transpiration rises into the atmosphere. There it forms clouds. Clouds may travel hundreds of kilometres. As the water vapour in the clouds cools, it **condenses** back to its liquid form. It then falls back to earth as rain, sleet or snow. Eventually this rain-water enters rivers, lakes and seas to begin the cycle again.

Not all water is the same. The elements hydrogen and oxygen combine to form the basis of all water (H_2O). But seawater contains other elements which give it its salty taste. River water and lake water do not contain as many **trace elements**.

More than 97 per cent of the Earth's waters are in the seas. Less than 3 per cent is fresh water. Yet it is this 3 per cent (found in rivers and lakes) that is most important to us. Only fresh water can be used by humans and only fresh water can irrigate our crops. Most animals and plants that live on land need fresh water. With so little fresh water in the world it is especially important for us to take good care to protect it from pollution.

Water is important in almost everything we do. We use it for transportation, irrigation and recreation. Manganese and other important minerals are taken from the ocean. Here women in Sri Lanka are collecting salt from the sea water. ▼

The Wet World

▲ Special submarines such as this enable scientists to study life deep under the sea. This vessel, called the 'Eared Octopus', is specially made to withstand the tremendous pressures found deep under the sea.

There are no boundaries between the oceans. All the oceans of the world are connected and flow into one another. They are all parts of one big ocean.

The Oceans

The oceans of the hydrosphere are the largest **biome** on the planet. Unlike the lithosphere, which is made up of many different biomes (such as deserts, mountains, rainforests), the oceans of the hydrosphere form a single biome. This biome is larger than all the biomes of the lithosphere put together. The surface area of the hydrosphere is more than twice as large as the surface area of the lithosphere. But this is only part of the story, because the hydrosphere is also much deeper than the lithosphere. The part of Earth on which land animals and plants live is very small. Most animals and plants live on the Earth's surface. Even when we consider the highest flying birds and the deepest burrowing animals, the region of life on the lithosphere is only a few

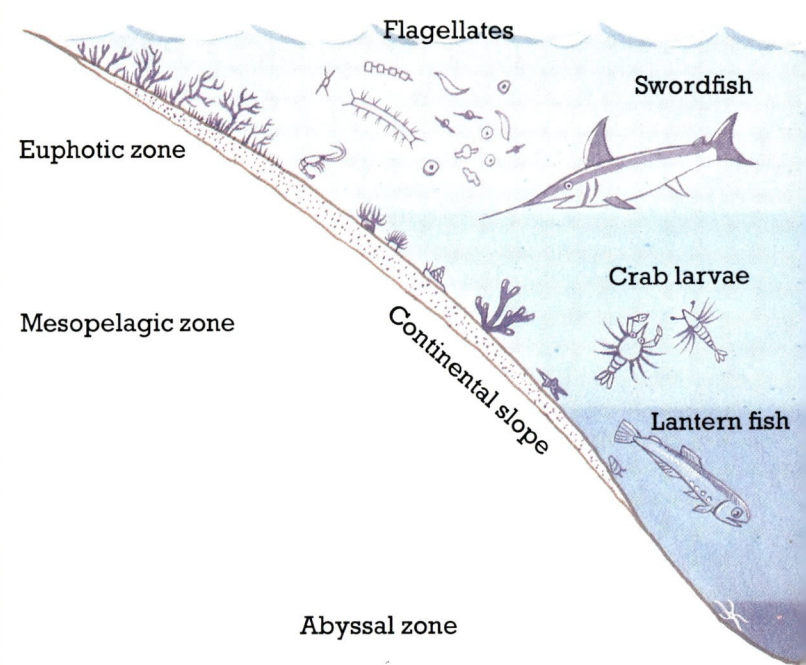

Flagellates

Swordfish

Euphotic zone

Crab larvae

Mesopelagic zone

Continental slope

Lantern fish

Abyssal zone

hundred metres thick. While the depth of the lithosphere can be measured in tens of metres, the oceans must be measured in kilometres. The average depth of the world's oceans is almost 4 kms (2.5 miles). Animals and plants live in all parts of the ocean. Some, like the jellyfish, live on the surface. Others, like most fish and **plankton**, inhabit the middle range. And at the bottom are sponges, corals, molluscs and many other kinds of seaplants and animals. There is no part of the hydrosphere without living things.

Life in the Oceans

In spite of its great size, the hydrosphere does not have very many different types of living things in it. Eighty per cent of the species of plants and animals on Earth are found in the lithosphere. The hydrosphere only has about 20 per cent of the Earth's life-forms, and these are not evenly distributed. Nine out of every ten species which live in the hydrosphere, live on the ocean floor.

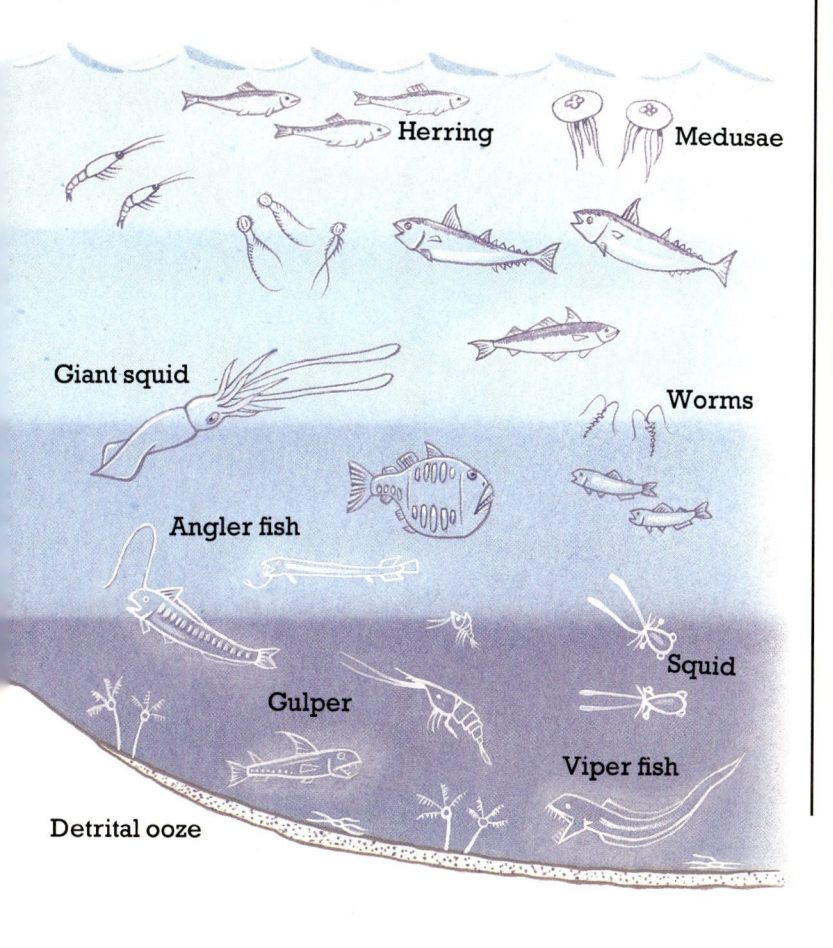

Herring

Medusae

Giant squid

Worms

Angler fish

Squid

Gulper

Viper fish

Detrital ooze

◀ **Ocean strata.** The ocean can be divided into different strata according to what lives there. In the uppermost stratum (the euphotic zone), sunlight still penetrates the water. The deepest (abyssal) zone is one of complete darkness where luminous fish and other animals have to make their own light.

Water Pollution

The hydrosphere is important for many reasons. It provides the water that is needed by all living things. Not only do we drink water but we also use fresh water to irrigate the land. This enables us to grow food without having to rely on rain. We can grow more food this way. Oceans, lakes and rivers are themselves important sources of food. Fish are the major source of protein for many people of the world. And, of course, much of our salt comes from the sea. Not only do we use salt to flavour our food but it is also an important natural **preservative**.

The oceans are also an important source of raw materials. Much of the world's crude oil and natural gas comes from beneath the sea-floor. Other minerals, such as manganese, are also mined from the sea. This is done by special vessels which dredge the ocean floor.

For all that we depend upon the hydrosphere, we treat it very badly. There are many ways in which we pollute the hydrosphere. For thousands of years we have used water to flush away human waste products. We use rivers as sewers to carry our waste away. We dump refuse into lakes and oceans. This waste is now building up to intolerable levels.

Human waste is not the only refuse we dump into the sea. Many industries dump unwanted chemicals and other dangerous substances

This barge is carrying waste material from New York out to sea, where it will be dumped. This is a very controversial event which happens daily. ▼

into rivers and seas. This is because it is cheaper to dump waste than to reprocess it to make it safe. These industrial wastes are called **effluents**.

Oil Slicks

Oil pollution is a major problem in the sea. Some oil is spilled by accident but much more oil is dumped in the ocean as waste. When oil is spilt or dumped on water it will float and form a slick. These can spread to cover a wide area and have a terrible effect on the environment. A spill from just one large tanker can kill 30,000 seabirds.

Dangerous chemicals can enter the hydrological cycle in other ways as well. Rain can wash away the chemicals that farmers use. These chemical fertilizers and pesticides may help their crops grow, but they are dangerous when they are washed into rivers and streams. When there are too many chemicals in the water it becomes unsafe. It may even become poisonous. These poisons do not only affect people. They can kill the plants and animals living in the water.

▲ The Nishua River in the USA looks peaceful, but waste products and pollution from a paper mill enter it from the pipe upstream, killing the aquatic life.

▲ The effects of pollution in the water can be catastrophic for the animals that live there.

The Future

People all over the world are dependent upon water. These people in China grow mulberry bushes to feed silk worms. To do this, they need to keep the bushes well irrigated. ▼

Polluting the hydrosphere endangers us all. We must take action to stop it getting worse. Happily there are ways of cleaning the waters. Sewage and other human waste can be treated before it is flushed into the rivers and seas. This treatment kills dangerous organisms in the sewage and makes it harmless. The sludge that is left can be safely dumped at sea. In this way some chemicals can also be made safe for dumping.

Dangerous Chemicals

Those chemicals that cannot be made safe by treatment, need special handling. Some dangerous chemicals can be made safe by burning them at very high temperatures. Special ships have been built that can do this far out at sea. Burning at sea this way, far from land, gives extra protection. Some especially dangerous materials like **toxic** chemicals and **radioactive** waste are put in special containers before they are dumped. It would be better if they were not dumped at all, but containers at least increase our safety. Measures such as these can help clean up the hydrosphere.

The Mediterranean Sea

The Mediterranean Sea was, until recently, badly polluted. Pollutants once dumped there are trapped for a long time because the sea is almost completely landlocked. About one hundred million people live along the coast. Most of their waste was pumped directly into

This sewage plant is designed to remove toxic waste. The treated sewage can then safely be flushed into the rivers and seas. ▶

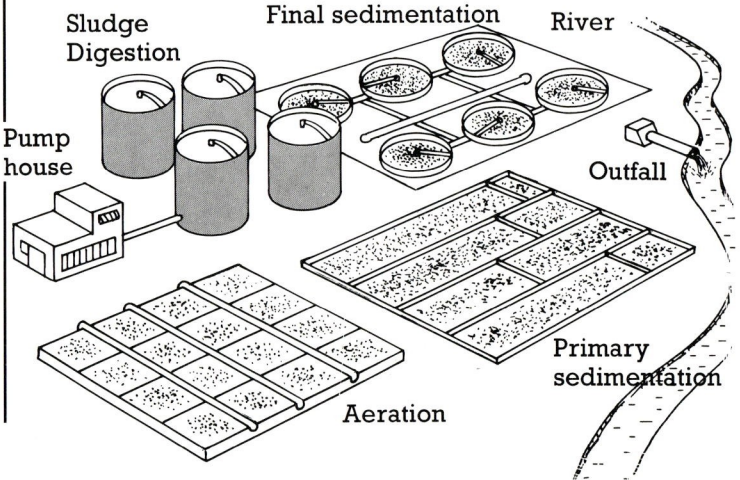

Sludge Digestion

Final sedimentation

River

Pump house

Outfall

Primary sedimentation

Aeration

the sea. The run-off of agricultural chemicals that were washed by rain into the rivers that feed the Mediterranean was another source of pollutants. Industrial dumping in the Mediterranean made the problem worse. The sea became so polluted that many beaches were declared unsafe. In some places it was dangerous to eat seafood, like mussels and clams, because they were badly contaminated.

For a time it seemed as if pollution was going to kill all life in the sea. But in 1975, the first steps were taken to stop the pollution. The countries that surround the Mediterranean made strict rules about dumping wastes. We can already see the results of their actions. Today there is less pollution entering the Mediterranean. As a result it is getting cleaner. But there is still a long way to go before we finish cleaning up the mess we have made.

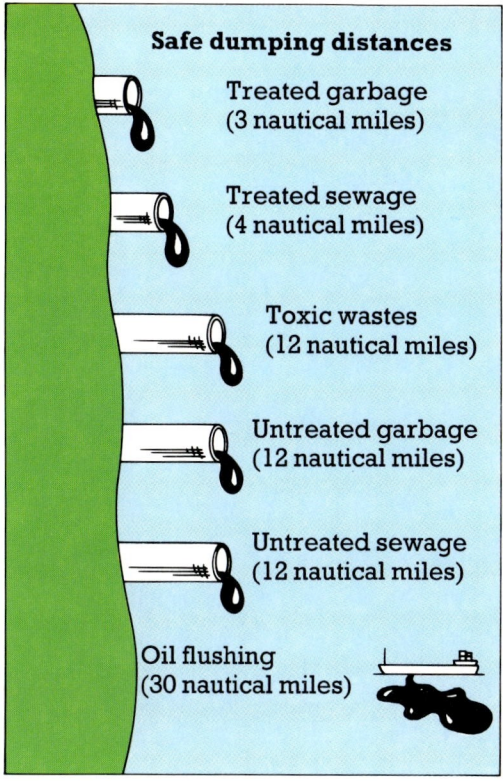

Safe dumping distances

Treated garbage
(3 nautical miles)

Treated sewage
(4 nautical miles)

Toxic wastes
(12 nautical miles)

Untreated garbage
(12 nautical miles)

Untreated sewage
(12 nautical miles)

Oil flushing
(30 nautical miles)

▲ This diagram shows the distances that the British government considers safe for dumping different types of waste material out at sea. These distances may vary according to laws in different countries.

A nautical mile is longer than an ordinary mile. It equals 1.85 km.

◀ Special measures can be taken to clean water that was once polluted. When the water is clean again and the source of pollution is stopped, it can be restocked with fish. This river has been cleaned up, and fish can once again thrive there. But the cost of carrying out schemes like this can be very high.

5: THE EMPTY QUARTER

The Deserts

Deserts are one the Earth's most distinctive biomes. They are also one of the largest. Natural deserts are found in the Earth's **arid** zones. These arid lands together with the semi-arid lands that border them cover one-third of the Earth's land surface.

Deserts have many distinctive characteristics. Their lack of people, their special vegetation, the absence of cultivated crops, extremes of temperature, and the low organic content of their soil have all been used to define deserts. But the most important definition of all is that deserts are arid. They are dry places. Deserts are places which receive less than 250 mm (10 inches) of rain each year. All other characteristics of a desert may be traced to this dryness.

World Map (showing the major desert regions – see page 40 for the regions under threat of desertification)

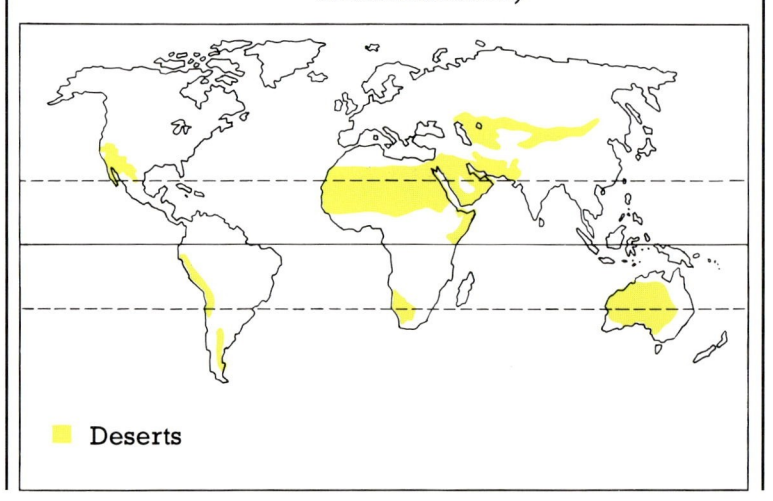

■ Deserts

The rainshadow. Moist air rises from the sea and falls as rain on the mountains. Very little of this moisture gets beyond and the land behind is said to be in a rainshadow.

Dry air

Moist air

Desert Temperatures

The aridity of desert environments has an effect on daily temperatures. In non-desert regions, humid air helps block some solar heat from reaching the ground during the day. Humid air also helps keep heat from escaping into the atmosphere at night. Because of this, places with humid climates have a smaller change in day and night temperature than deserts. As a result, deserts suffer from extremes of temperature. In the **tropics**, deserts can get very hot during the day and then get very cold at night. In some desert areas, the temperature may change by as much as 38 degrees centigrade (100 degrees Fahrenheit) between day and night.

Plant Life

Plants have to be particularly hardy to survive these harsh conditions. They must also adapt to a very short growing season. This is true both in tropical deserts and in **tundra** regions. In the hot deserts of the tropical and sub-tropical regions, plants only grow when the rains come. This may happen as a single terrific thunderstorm between years of drought. In the polar deserts, there are only a few months each year when the temperature is above freezing. It is only in these short periods that plants can grow.

▲ Rain comes only infrequently to the desert. But when it does come the result can be astounding. This is a photograph of the Kalahari Desert after a rain storm.

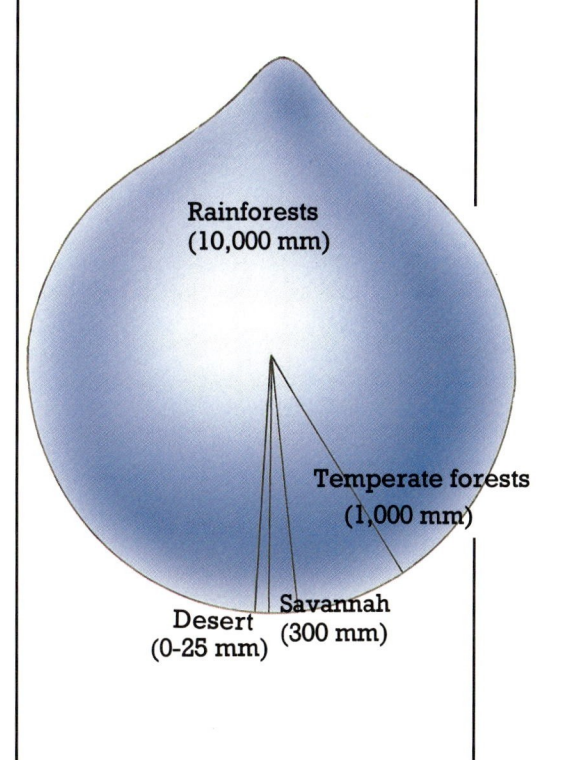

Rainforests
(10,000 mm)

Temperate forests
(1,000 mm)

Savannah
(300 mm)

Desert
(0-25 mm)

▲ Annual rainfall distribution in different environments.

Types of Desert

We usually think of deserts as having sand dunes like these, but most do not. Only a fraction of the world's deserts are covered by shifting sand dunes. ▼

There are several different kinds of desert. They are all arid and all have sparse plant and animal life. Tropical and sub-tropical deserts are most familiar to us. Tropical deserts have only one season and are hot all year round. Sub-tropical deserts may have seasons, but they are very extreme. Summers in sub-tropical deserts are short and very hot. Winters are very long and cold.

Polar Deserts

Some deserts are covered in ice. Like other deserts, they get very little **precipitation** each year. But because it is below freezing almost all the time, what snow and ice there is, never melts away. There are two kinds of cold desert. Tundra deserts have a short summer season when the temperature climbs above freezing. Melting ice provides enough water for hardy plants to grow. In polar deserts, the temperature is below freezing all year round. Not only is the ground permanently frozen but so too is all the water. Because there is no water available to plants, there is almost no vegetation in the polar deserts. The Antarctic is a polar desert.

Interior Deserts

All natural deserts suffer from the lack of moisture. There are three reasons why their air is dry. Some deserts are far from the sea. Evaporation from the oceans provides most of the moisture in the air. Lands which are far from the sea do not benefit from this moist air. It falls as precipitation before it gets to the distant lands. Deserts of this kind are called continental interior deserts. The Gobi Desert of Inner Asia is a desert of this kind.

A second cause of dry air can be found in the world climate system. The circulation of the Earth's wind and weather follows a regular pattern. Some areas receive a lot of rain each year. Other areas do not. Some deserts are in areas where the wind is dry all year round. The Sahara and the Rub'al Khali Desert of Saudi Arabia are deserts of this kind.

A third cause of dry air comes because of rainshadows. Some deserts are in regions where warm, moist air must cross a mountain chain. As it rises to cross the mountains the air cools. This causes the moisture in the air to condense and precipitation occurs over the mountains. The air which comes down on the other side of the mountain has lost its moisture. Lands in the ''shadow'' of the mountains get only dry air, not rain. The Patagonian Desert in Argentina is a rain-shadow desert.

▲ Stony deserts like this one in Namibia are common around the world. The great Gobi Desert is also a stony desert.

Polar deserts are very inhospitable places. The temperature is below freezing almost all year round and they get very little precipitation. Polar deserts can be covered in snow because while only a bit falls each year, it never melts. Year after year these small amounts of snow build up. ▼

Marginal Lands

The Mongols and the Kazakhs are two of the peoples who live on the steppes of Siberia and Inner Asia. They live as nomadic cowboys whose herds eat the lush grass of the steppes. ▼

There is little that can be done about the world's natural deserts. These extemely arid zones are the result of climatic conditions and natural forces beyond human control. Of greater concern is the state of the world's semi-arid regions. These are lands which receive more rainfall than deserts but not enough for forests or crops to grow naturally. Semi-arid lands are, typically, grasslands. They are often called **marginal** lands.

Grasslands

Semi-arid grasslands are an important biome. There are two main types of grassland: **savannah** and **steppe**. Savannahs are grassy plains of the tropical and subtropical regions. They are found primarily in Africa and South America. Steppes are also grassy plains but they are in temperate regions. The main steppe areas are in Russia, Siberia and Inner Asia. Steppes have hot summers and cold winters. Savannahs do not show much seasonal variation in temperature. They may, however, have wet and dry seasons.

The grasses form a thick blanket of vegetation which protects the soil. These grasses can grow quite tall. The people of Mongolia, a country made up of the steppe, have a saying about their grass. They say it was so tall that they could not see their animals until the wind

blew it down. Grasses like this make good food for grazing animals. Because they can be used for grazing, grasslands are often called rangelands.

Food Crops

Semi-arid lands are marginal in two senses. First, they exist on the margins of deserts. That is, they are a buffer zone between deserts and wetter areas. Semi-arid lands are also marginal in the sense that they can support some agricultural activity if it is carefully managed. Food crops can be grown on marginal lands with careful irrigation. It is necessary to rotate crops and leave long **fallow** periods so that the soil is not exhausted. If care is not taken, all the nutrients in the soil may be used up. When this happens, crops will not grow and land becomes more like desert.

These marginal lands are very important. They provide the world with up to 20 per cent of its food supplies. Seven hundred million people live in these areas. More than 200 million of them are in danger because grasslands are being destroyed.

▲ The savannah-lands of Kenya are lush green places during the wet season. Many wild animals will come to this waterhole to drink at nightfall.

Upsetting the Balance

The Dust Bowl

In the United States earlier this century, new kinds of tractors made it possible for the first time to plough through the thick prairie grasses of the Great Plains. Land that was formerly used only for grazing was ploughed up and planted with crops like wheat and maize. The result was erosion on a massive scale. Vast areas of land became barren. This was called the American dust bowl. Huge clouds of soil were blown out to sea. These clouds were so thick that they blackened the sky. Millions of tonnes of soil were lost. This attempt to farm marginal land ruined it not only for farming but for grazing, too. It was one of the biggest environmental disasters the world had ever seen.

The grasslands can be very productive when managed carefully. While they are not very good for farming, they can provide excellent pastures for livestock. Nomads have been particularly good at using this pasture. They move from one place to another in order to find food and water for their livestock. As long as the animals do not stay in one place for too long, they do not harm the grassland environment. Problems occur when the livestock eat all the vegetative cover. When bare soil is exposed to the wind and rain, erosion takes place. This is happening in many parts of the world today.

Population Growth

Increasing populations around the world mean that farmers need to produce more crops. One way they do this is by developing new land. Because all the good land is already being used for crops, farmers turn to marginal lands. They convert grassland for crops. This is bad for the pastoralists because it takes some of their best pasture away. There is less pasture available for their livestock. More animals have to exist on less land. This is bad for the grassland environment. In a short time, the over-grazed pasture can turn to desert. This is happening in almost every country where livestock graze grasslands.

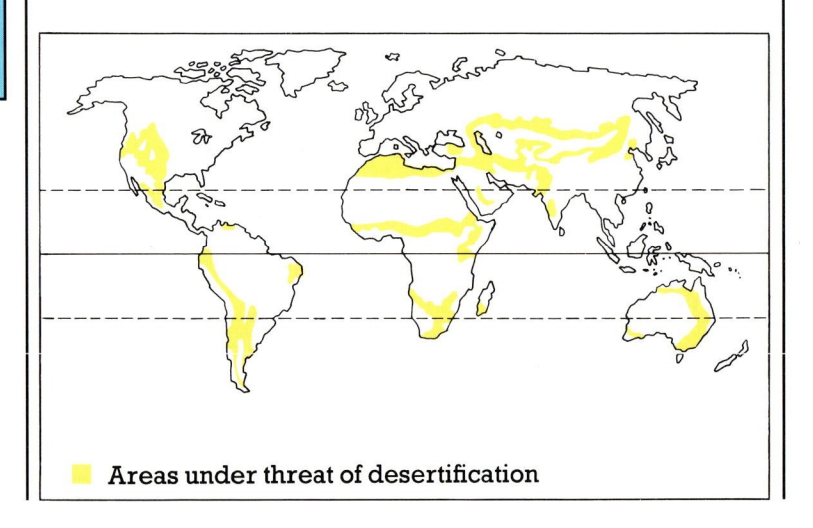

■ **Areas under threat of desertification**

This map shows the main areas of the world under threat of desertification (see also the map on page 34). ▶

Soil Exhaustion

Changing the best grassland to farmland also causes other erosion problems. Marginal lands are not really suited to farming. Taking away the protective cover of grass makes them vulnerable to erosion. Grassland soils are also too thin for farming. Crops can only grow on them for a few years before the soil is exhausted.

▲ Nomads are people who live in the desert. They move their herds of livestock from place to place in order to find food for their animals. In many places in the world they have been doing this for hundreds of years. Today, suitable land for their animals to graze on is becoming harder to find. ▼

Stopping the Advance

Getting water from the desert is a great problem. These people are building a deep well. ▶

Natural climate changes can lead to the growth of deserts. There is nothing we can do about this. But desertification, the turning of good land into deserts, is something we can stop. Humans are the cause of desertification. They can also be its cure. In a hungry world it is essential that we conserve our soil resources. We will only have enough food for the Earth's population if we ensure there is enough land on which to grow it. Soil is our most precious non-renewable resource. Erosion is the major threat to it. One hundred and twenty thousand square kilometres (12 million hectares) are destroyed by erosion every year. Sixty per cent of this erosion occurs in grasslands which are turned to desert. When this happens we lose valuable pasture for the world's livestock.

The Green Great Wall

Older forest

Encroaching
Gobi Desert

Recently planted
forest

CHINA

Deserts get bigger

Deserts can advance quite rapidly. Each year the edge of the Sahara Desert moves as much as 10kms (6 miles). Desertification spreads like a rash. Over-cultivation and over-grazing causes a small patch of desert to appear. This puts more pressure on the remaining good land. Soon more and more patches of desert break out. As the number of desert patches increases, so they begin to link up. A whole region can turn to desert.

Changing Farming Patterns

Desertification occurs because of bad farming and herding practices. It is the misuse of land which allows deserts to expand. Land on the margins of the deserts is particularly at risk. Cutting down trees and destroying the protective grass cover allows sand to blow over fields. Erosion of the grassland soil may lead it to becoming desert itself.

The Green Great Wall

Conservation efforts are also underway in other temperate forests of the world. Northern China was deforested long ago to make way for agriculture. Now erosion is a big problem there. To combat this the Chinese are planting a Green Great Wall of trees. In this massive **afforestation** effort, the Chinese plan to plant millions of trees in broad bands stretching across the entire country.

Dangerous Goats!

The best way to stop the desert's advance is to change farming and herding methods. Over-cultivation and over-grazing are the two biggest problems. Care can be taken to stop farmers from changing grassland to cropland. Herd sizes must be reduced. Grasslands can only be protected when the size of herds is in balance with the capacity of the land to safely feed them. Care must be taken in the selection of what kind of livestock to raise. Goats, which are among the hardiest kinds of livestock, are particularly bad for the marginal land environment. They will eat everything. This puts a tremendous strain on the soil and exposes it to erosion. In vulnerable areas goats can be a disaster.

◀ Goats cause terrible damage. After eating all the vegetation from the ground, this Moroccan goat climbed a tree to get more food. Yet they are a common animal amongst nomads.

6: THE GREEN BLANKET

The World's Forests

This map shows where the main areas of rainforest are found. ▶

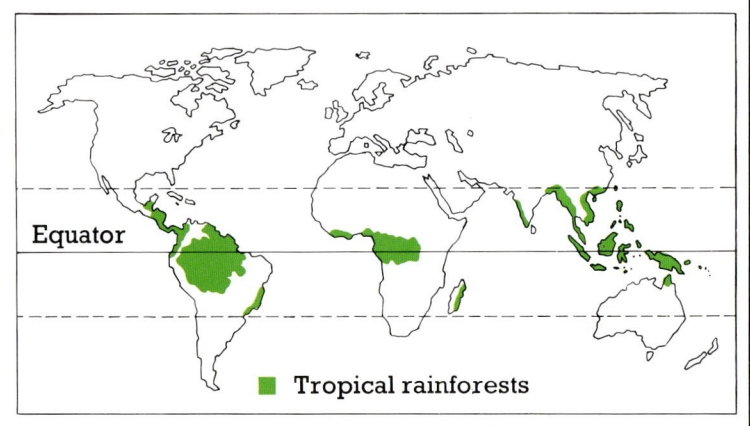

Equator

■ Tropical rainforests

Facts & Feats

● The oldest living thing on Earth is the bristlecone pine of the North American Rocky Mountains. They can live to be 4,600 years old. This means they were alive when the Egyptian pyramids were built.

● The world's largest tree is also found in North America. A giant redwood (sequoia) there, named the General Sherman, is almost 92 metres (300 feet) high and 35 metres (115 feet) in circumference.

● Trees are the tallest living things. The tallest tree ever measured was a douglas fir in British Columbia. It grew to a height of 126 metres (415 feet).

● The tallest tree growing today is a mountain ash which stands 99 metres (325 feet) high in Tasmania.

● The coniferous forest of Siberia is the world's largest forest. It covers an area of 1.2 billion hectares (3 billion acres). This is 25 per cent of the world's total forest area.

Forests cover about one-fifth of the Earth's land surface. They are important for many reasons. Forests affect the air we breathe. They affect the weather. They are the source of our timber, one of the most important raw materials. They are also home to thousands of other plants and animals. Many of these are also important to us. Twenty-five per cent of our medicines come from forest plants.

Forests Make Oxygen

Forests are an important source of oxygen, an essential element for life. A characteristic of plants is that they breathe in carbon dioxide and give off oxygen. This oxygen is released into the atmosphere where it is an important part of the air we breathe.

Trees play several different roles in the water cycle. Tree roots help bind the soil together. This traps rainwater and slows it down, so that it can be absorbed by the soil. When water is absorbed in this way, it can be held for the plant's future use. Rapid erosion can occur when there are no roots to bind the soil. In rainforests, the canopy of leaves acts as a great, green umbrella which protects the forest floor from the harsh tropical sun and the torrential tropical rains. Without them, the jungle soil would soon wash away.

Recycling water

Trees also help recycle water in another way. Moisture which falls as rain is recycled by plants back into the atmosphere by the process of transpiration. Transpiration helps keep the leaves cool. It also helps the plant's absorption of nutrients from the soil. Plants take up water from the ground through their roots and release it back into the atmosphere through their leaves. The water vapour released from plants then forms clouds which can then fall back to Earth again as rain. This process is repeated again and again in a continuous cycle.

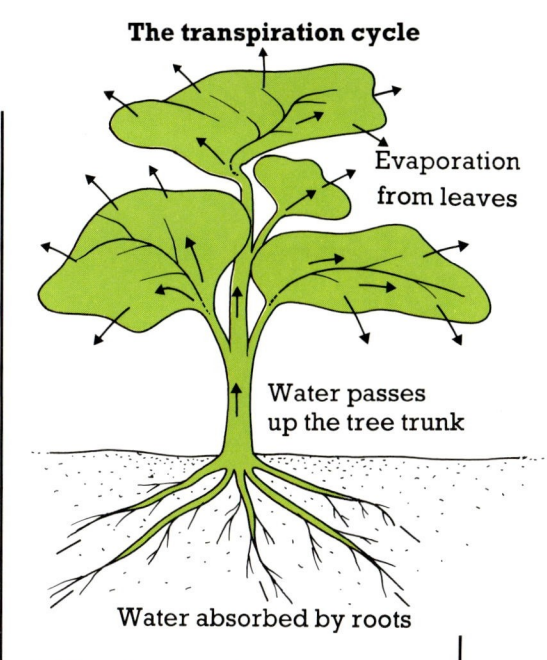

The transpiration cycle

Evaporation from leaves

Water passes up the tree trunk

Water absorbed by roots

▲ This diagram shows how trees and plants recycle water. They take it in through their roots and release it into the air through their leaves.

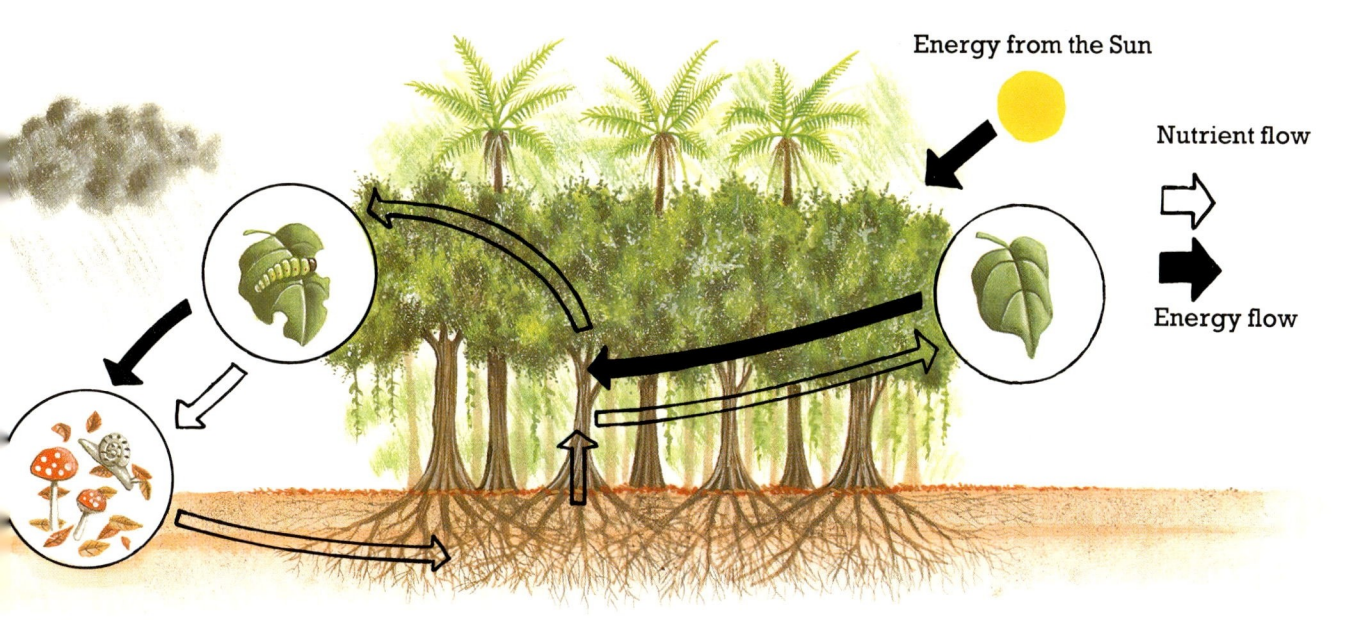

Energy from the Sun

Nutrient flow

Energy flow

▲ **The Rainforest Ecosystem.** Nutrients and energy are constantly recycled in the rainforest ecosystem.

◀ Clouds of mist hanging over the hill forests of Peru – one stage in the water cycle.

Different Forests

There are three main types of forest. Each is home to different plants and animals.

Tropical Rainforests

In the tropics, where temperatures are hot all year round and where there is a high rainfall every year, dense jungles – called tropical rainforests – are common. About half of the world's forests are tropical rainforests. They cover about 10 per cent of the Earth's land surface. The main rainforest areas are parts of Central and South America, Central and West Africa, and Southeast Asia. Tropical forests are different from other forests in several ways. First, they are far wetter than other forests. This is because they are in places that have very heavy rains. Rainforests are also much more dense than other forests. Several thousand different varieties of tree may exist in a single rainforest. Their trees have broad leaves and are green all year.

Temperate Forests

In lands where a cold winter interrupts the growing season there is less rainfall and the temperature is cooler than in rainforests. Forests called temperate forests grow here. The trees have broad leaves and shed them once a year. Europe and the eastern half of North America were once covered with vast temperate forests. Most of these were cut down in the 18th and 19th centuries to make way for agriculture and industry.

Squirrel monkey

Jaguar

Different Tree Types

Coniferous trees

Temperate forest trees

Rainforest trees

Coniferous Forests

A third type of forest can be found where the winter is very long and cold and where the growing season is very short. These are coniferous forests. Coniferous (cone-bearing) trees are especially suited for these harsh conditions. They have small needle-shaped leaves which stay green all year round. Their seeds are very tough. Although coniferous forests may be quite large they have very few different types of trees.

▲ Coniferous trees have needle-like leaves which stay green all year. Temperate forest trees have broad leaves which usually turn brown and fall off each year. Rainforest trees have broad leaves which stay on all the time.

Anaconda

Slipper orchid

White-tailed trogon

Bar-tailed trogon

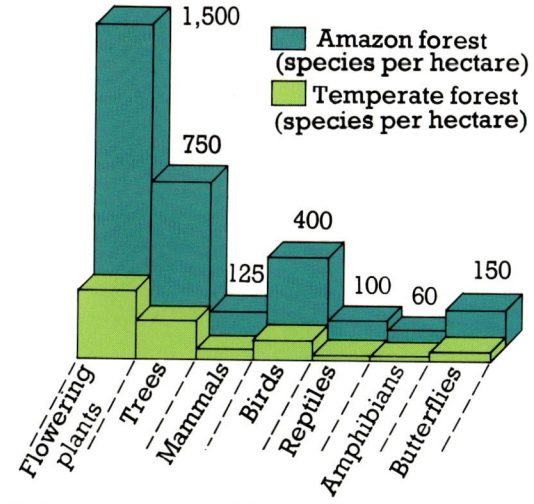

■ Amazon forest (species per hectare)
■ Temperate forest (species per hectare)

1,500
750
400
125
100
60
150

Flowering plants · Trees · Mammals · Birds · Reptiles · Amphibians · Butterflies

◄ These are some of the beautiful plants and animals of the rainforest.

47

Cutting down Trees

▲ Bulldozers cut roads into even the deepest rainforests. Once there are roads, farmers come to make fields and to graze their animals. Once a rainforest is opened this way, its fragile ecosystem is easily destroyed.

Each year the population of the Earth grows. Each year more food has to be grown. Each year farmers, like this one in Morocco, cut further into the forest to make new fields to grow that food. ▶

Deforestation is the destruction of forests. All over the world forests are being cut down.

Losing Forests

In Europe and the Middle East, where great numbers of people have lived for thousands of years, there are very few forests left. Lebanon once had vast cedar forests. So important was the cedar tree that it is the emblem on their flag. Yet today hardly a single cedar remains in Lebanon. England, too, was once covered by magnificent forests. In medieval times the kings of England hunted wild animals in the forests that covered the southern counties like a green blanket. Today those forests too have disappeared. North America was covered by some of the largest forests the world has ever seen. Yet by 1860, 90 per cent of the forests in the United States had been cut down.

Not all deforestation went on in the distant past. Some of the worst cases of deforestation are going on today. It is especially bad in the tropical rainforests. Since the beginning of this century almost half the world's rainforests have been cut down. Those that remain are being torn up at a rate of 40 hectares (100

acres) every minute. This means that a forest the size of football pitch disappears every second. Put another way, every month a forest the size of Wales is destroyed.

Forests are cut down for many reasons. Wood is a valuable material. It can be used in many ways. It can also be burned. In many countries wood is an important source of fuel for cooking and heating.

Not all forests are cut down because people want their wood. Forests are also cut down to clear a space for farmers to grow their crops or graze their animals. They are also cut down to make room for new towns and cities. And for the roads that connect them.

Losing Precious Soil
Rapid deforestation causes many problems. Without tree roots to bind the soil it is easily eroded. Fierce tropical rains can wash unprotected soil away. When these forests are destroyed, it is not only the trees that die. The whole ecosystem is thrown out of balance. Other forest plants and animals also die.

▲ People have since earliest times needed wood – to build houses, furniture or boats. It has been an important source of fuel throughout our history.

▲ Baskets of firewood for sale in Nepal. Firewood is a cheap source of fuel for the people who live here, but its collection is causing the destruction of whole forests and ecosystems.

Saving the Trees

▲ This papaw comes from South America, growing in the forest. The fruit is orange-coloured and edible. Like other useful plants, it could come under threat if its habitat is destroyed.

The Rainforest Floor. Rainforest soil is very thin. Most of the nutrients in it come from the leaf and plant litter which blanket it. ▶

Deforestation may occur for many reasons. The demand for fuel, timber and new land for farming puts great pressure on the world's forests. The temperate forests of Europe and North America were the first to suffer severe deforestation. Most of the European forests were destroyed long ago to meet the demand for farm land and raw materials. Over half the forests of the eastern United States were destroyed for the same reason. In these areas we have learned our lesson and forests are now protected. Great efforts are made to plant new ones.

Today, the situation with the world's rainforests is the greatest cause for concern. Once they are destroyed, rainforests are gone for ever. Unlike temperate forests, it is impossible to replant a rainforest. We cannot recreate the diversity of life in them.

Not only are the tropical rainforests at risk. So, too, is the land on which they grow. Despite their luxurious growth, most tropical forest soils are very poor. Few of the nutrients used by tropical plants come from the soil. Most come from dead and rotting vegetation on the forest floor. The jungle floor is like a vast **compost heap**. This layer of debris may be only a few centimetres thick. Nevertheless it is the source of most essential nutrients.

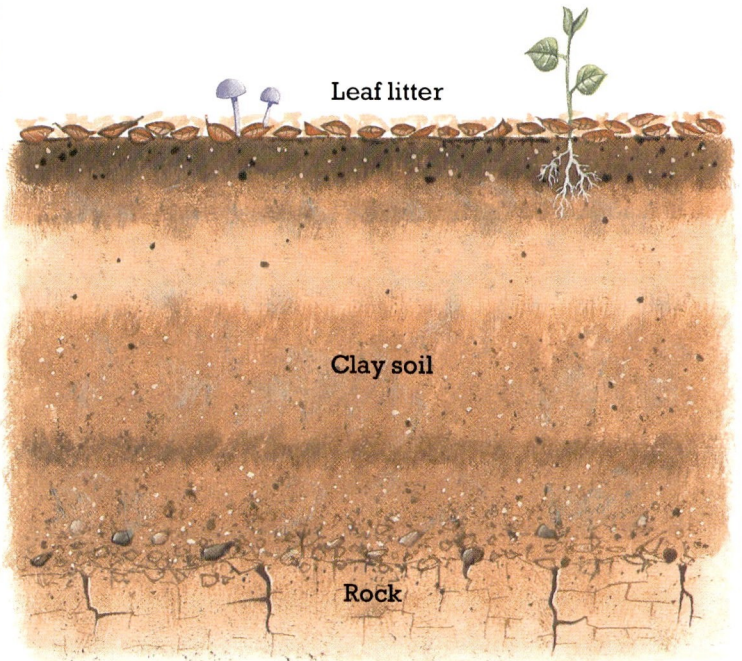

Leaf litter

Clay soil

Rock

◀ This forest in Brazil was cut down for its timber. Tiny seedlings are being replanted in the hope of starting a new forest and protecting the soil from the fierce tropical rains.

The debris that covers the forest floor is quickly broken down and recycled. Dead plant material soon becomes food for the living. The warm, humid conditions speed the decay. When left undisturbed the rainforest is an almost perfectly closed ecosystem. Ninety-nine per cent of the goodness in the plants is recycled. But cutting down the trees destroys this carefully balanced environment. The chief source of nutrients disappears. All that remains is the thin soil. This soil is so poor that plants cannot grow on it. Without plants to cover it, wind and water soon erode it away. Under these conditions it takes only a few years for rainforest to turn to desert.

Hugging Trees

In northern India, deforestation is also a problem. There the people are trying to stop it before it gets too bad. Members of the Chipko Movement hug the trees in an attempt to prevent them from being cut down. They hope to stop wood-cutters getting near the trees with axes and saws. They are protecting their environment.

This re-afforestation programme is carefully controlled. ▼

7: WILDLIFE

New Species

Guenon monkeys

▲ These rare guenon monkeys come from Madagascar.

The rosy periwinkle, one of the newly-discovered miracle plants from the Amazon rainforest. ▼

No one knows exactly how many different species of plants and animals there are on Earth. We do know that scientists have identified around 15 million species so far. Many more are still to be discovered.

Most of the species of the world that remain unknown are insects and plants. Most of these are to be found in the tropics. Rainforests are the chief source of unknown species. Fewer than half the species of the rainforests have been discovered and studied by scientists.

Untapped Sources

The diversity of wildlife is important for other reasons. It represents a vast storehouse of future products. So far this storehouse has been hardly touched. We know about only a tiny fraction of the plants in the Amazon jungle.

Yet the unknown plants may be very important. Today, 40 per cent of our medicines come from plants. New discoveries are being made almost every day. The rosy periwinkle has been found to be a cure for some kinds of cancer. Who knows what secrets the other thousands of plant species hold in store?

Plants for Medicine

Plants are not only important for food and medicines. New discoveries are being made in other areas as well. Another plant of the Amazon has been called the "petrol plant" because it provides a fluid that can be used in place of petrol in car engines. This plant may someday supply a renewable source of fuel to replace our shrinking fossil fuel resources. The jojoba plant of the North American deserts is another important discovery. This plant produces a very fine oil. It is now being used as a substitute for whale oil in many industries. This plant may help prevent the extinction of the whale.

There are many discoveries still to be made. If we get the chance. One of the worrying things is that many wild plants and animals are disappearing before we even discover them. They are being made **extinct**. This is one of the worst environmental problems facing us today.

The jojoba plant grows in North American deserts. The berries produce a very valuable oil. In some cases, it is replacing whale oil. ▼

Wildlife under Threat

Animal extinction since 1650

Wildlife everywhere is under threat. Many species of plant or animal have become extinct. Most often this is because of human activities – hunting or changing environments.

Extinction

Extinction is happening today at a rate faster than ever before. In the 400 years between 1550 and 1950 an average of one species a year was made extinct by humans. By 1985, the rate had increased to almost one species each day. At this rate of increase 50,000 species per year could be lost by the end of the century. Put another way, more than 100 species each day will be lost in the year 2000. Many species are doomed unless we do something soon. In the

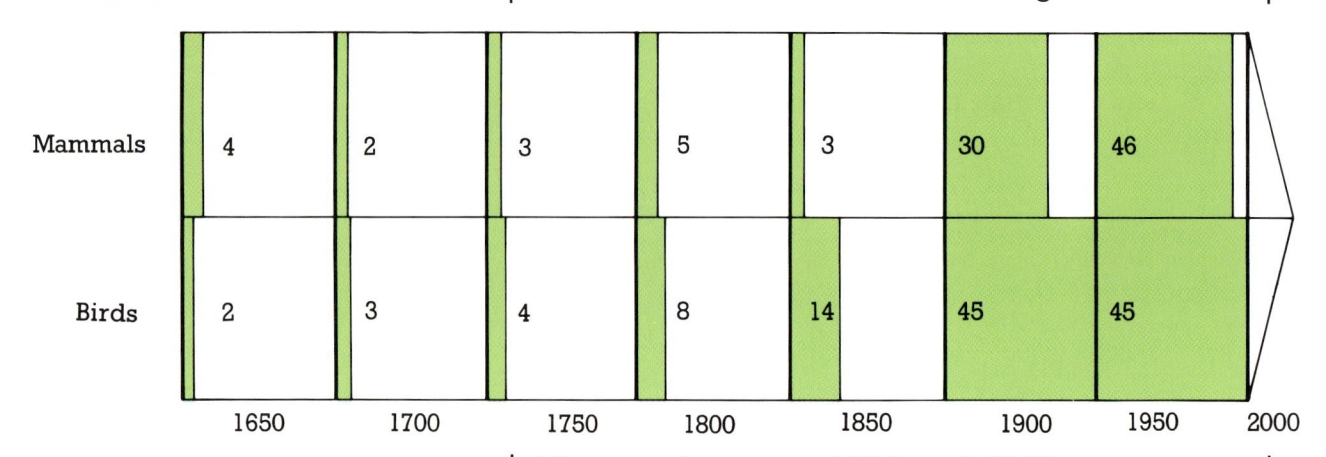

	1650	1700	1750	1800	1850	1900	1950	2000
Mammals	4	2	3	5	3	30	46	
Birds	2	3	4	8	14	45	45	

▲ This time line shows how many different types of birds and mammals became extinct in different periods from 1650 up to the present day.

20 years between 1980 and 2000 as many as 500,000 plant and animal species are expected to disappear. This is about 10 per cent of all the plant and animal species on Earth.

Not only is the pace of extinction changing, so too is the location of where it happens. In the past, most extinctions caused by humans occurred among small isolated communities of animals or plants. Usually these communities were on islands where the balance of nature was very fragile. When humans came to these islands they disrupted the balance. The dodo was hunted to extinction by hungry sailors who landed on Mauritius. Native animal species often had no defences against new species brought by people. The sheep, pigs, cattle and rabbits introduced by the colonizers of

Did You Know?

Extinction rates vary around the world. More species are under threat in some regions than in others. Asia has the most serious problem. A third of the Asian mammal species are in danger. The situation is best in Australia. There only 7 per cent of the mammal species are under threat. But even this is not good enough.

many islands often replaced native species of animals and made them extinct.

The arrival of ships brought another unwelcome visitor to the islands – rats. Rats quickly wiped out whole species of ground-dwelling birds by eating their eggs. They also made other smaller animals extinct.

Today the situation has changed. It is not just small, isolated, island communities which are threatened with extinction. There are animal and plant species on every continent, now under threat. Species of the tropical rain-forests and of the grasslands are particularly at risk.

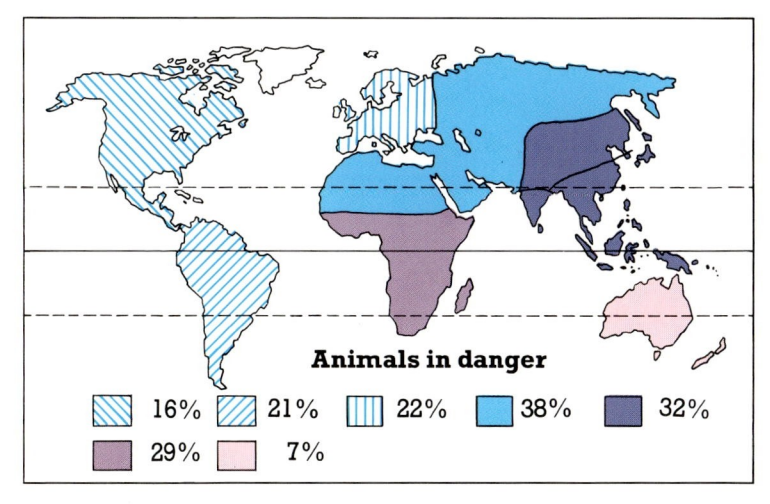

Animals in danger

16%		21%		22%		38%		32%
29%		7%						

The dodo (last seen on the island of Mauritius in 1700)

▲ The dodo and the passenger pigeon are just two kinds of birds which have been made extinct.

◀ **Endangered Species.** Plants and animals of all kinds – birds, mammals, reptiles, fish and insects – are under the threat of extinction. ▼

Humpback whale

Large blue butterfly

Panda

White rhinoceros

Californian condor

Snake's head fritillary

Extinction

▲ The North American bison (the buffalo) once covered the Great Plains in huge herds. They were hunted almost to extinction in the 19th century.

Bamboo and the Panda

Although it is the loss of large animals such as whales, tigers or eagles that makes the news, it is the loss of plant species which is most worrying. The extinction of a single plant species may threaten up to 40 other species of insects, animals and even other plants which are dependent on it. The giant panda faces extinction for this reason. Its food is a single species of bamboo. The demand for farm land means that there is less area in which the bamboo can grow. If the bamboo becomes extinct, so will the panda.

Most extinctions today are caused by human activities, mainly through hunting, competition, and habitat-destruction.

Hunting

Animals are hunted for food and for sport. Over-hunting can cause extinction. We have already seen what has happened to the dodo. Today, several species of whale have been hunted to near extinction. Hunters for sport can also cause extinctions. The North American bison once lived in huge herds hundreds of miles wide. They were all but wiped out by sportsmen. Today, the bustard (a bird) is threatened by Arab hunters in a similar way.

Animals are over-hunted for other reasons as well. Tigers, leopards and other big cats are threatened with extinction because their fur is valued for coats. Certain snake, crocodile and alligator species are threatened because their skin is used for shoes, gloves and handbags. Tortoiseshell is used for jewellery. Rhinoceros horn is valued for decoration and as a drug. The list of threatened species is endless.

Wildlife is also threatened by bringing new species into the environment. These new species compete with the native species. When this happens, native plants and animals can be wiped out. Sometimes people bring new species into an environment by accident. This happened with the rats off ships. Sometimes new species are introduced on purpose. Cats were brought to islands to keep down the rats. But the cats caused new problems for the native species as they, too, ate the native ground-dwelling birds. When sheep, pigs, goats, cattle or rabbits are introduced, they compete with native species.

Changing Habitats

The biggest cause of extinctions is habitat change. Cutting down rainforests and clearing grasslands for farming results in a massive destruction of wildlife. Many species are limited to a single habitat. When this habitat is changed, they die. Even small changes in the habitat can have a big effect. The wild bird population of England has been seriously decreased by the digging up of hedgerows. When the hedgerows disappear so, too, do the forms of wildlife that live in them.

▲ Luxury furs and reptile skins are fashion items which can result in the animals being hunted to extinction.

Facts & Feats

● Some scientists believe that it was an ancestor of the rat which made dinosaurs extinct. They say that these prehistoric rats ate the dinosaurs' eggs.

● Over-hunting has been a problem since humans first walked on earth. Woolly mammoths, camels and mastodons once roamed North America. Some scientists believe that they were made extinct by Stone Age people over-hunting.

● Today nearly 1,000 different kinds of animals and 20,000 kinds of plants face the threat of extinction.

● Ninety per cent of African rhinos have been killed since 1970. Some species are almost extinct. In Java there are only about 50 Javanese rhinos still alive.

◄ Many kinds of whales have been hunted almost to extinction. While most nations of the world have stopped hunting whales, Japan and Russia still continue to do so.

The Future

Old Faithful Geyser in Yellowstone National Park, Wyoming, USA, shoots boiling water high into the air. Yellowstone was the world's first conservation area. Now there are more than a thousand in countries all around the world. These conservation areas are important for the health of our planet. ▶

National Parks

Yellowstone National Park in the United States was the world's first conservation area. It was established in 1872. Now there are over 1,200 such parks and reserves in the world. In Africa, Kenya and Tanzania lead the way. Their parks not only preserve and protect but also earn money. Wildlife parks such as these attract many tourists. In Kenya, they have learned that a live lion is worth many times more than a dead one.

It is important that we stop the destruction of species. The health of the biosphere depends on it.

Saving the Environment

The greatest threat to species is the destruction of their habitat by humans. Safe-guarding the habitat is the first and most important step we can take. We can do this through better management of the land. Deforestation and desertification can and must be stopped. We cannot continue to destroy marginal lands. Humans must learn to use good farmland more efficiently. Species loss will not be stopped until human expansion is controlled.

Conservation areas, wildlife reserves and game parks are important ways of protecting animals and plants. By setting aside land for these areas they can be kept in their wild state. Hunters and developers must be kept out of these areas.

Zoos, botanical gardens and rare-breed centres are another way of protecting animal and plant species. While they do not protect the habitat, they are able to preserve at least some kinds of threatened wildlife. They are particularly important in those cases where it is not yet possible to save the natural habitat from destruction.

Zoos have had some dramatic successes. The European bison became extinct in the wild during the First World War. But a few survived in zoos. Recently they have been set free in the Bialowieza National Park in Poland. It is hoped that they will again establish themselves there in the wild. A similar experiment is being tried with a species of antelope that was over-hunted in its native Arabia. Antelope kept alive in zoos have bred and provided new young which have been re-introduced into Arabia.

Conservation laws also help protect wildlife. These laws prohibit the hunting, collecting or sale of endangered species.

▲ The European bison, once almost extinct, has now been re-established in the Bialowieza National Park in Poland. But success stories such as this are rare. Many plant and animal species will not be so lucky.

Wildlife reserves, like national parks, are special areas where plants and animals are protected. Reserves like this one in Africa are often the last hope for some species hunted to near extinction. ▼

Glossary

Acid: A class of chemicals that have several common characteristics. They contain hydrogen, neutralize alkalis, corrode metals, can be highly poisonous and turn blue litmus paper red.

Acid rain: Precipitation that contains a high acid content is called ''acid rain''. Acid rain occurs when pollutants, such as sulphur dioxide and nitrous oxides, combine with water vapour in the atmosphere.

Afforestation: Planting trees to make a forest.

Arid: Dry, parched or barren. The arid regions of the world are those areas that receive little rainfall. They include deserts.

Atmosphere: The layer of gases around a planet. The atmosphere of Earth is made up mainly of the gases nitrogen and oxygen as well as tiny amounts of neon, argon, carbon dioxide and other gases.

Bacterium (sing.), **bacteria** (pl.): Microscopic, one-celled organisms. They are found in the air, water and earth and in living and dead bodies.

Biome: An ecological community; a biological zone.

Biosphere: The regions of the Earth in which living things are found. The biosphere is made up of three different zones: the lithosphere (or land zone), the atmosphere (or air zone) and the hydrosphere (or water zone).

Chemicals: Substances which are made by, or used in, chemistry.

Combustion: The process of burning, giving off light and heat.

Compost: A mixture of decayed leaves, grass, and other organic materials used as fertilizer.

Condensation: The change of gas or vapour into a liquid. Condensation is the opposite of **evaporation**.

Contour ploughing: Tilling the soil in such a way that the ploughing follows the natural contours of the land. Ploughing in this way reduces erosion of the soil.

Desertification: An extreme form of environmental damage; the process by which productive land is turned into desert.

Drainage: The removal of excess water through pipes, channels and canals.

Effluent: Sewage; waste products, especially from factories and sewage works, that are pumped into rivers, lakes and seas.

Environment: Our surroundings; the circumstances and conditions which effect the way a person, animal or plant lives.

Erosion: The gradual wearing away of the Earth's surface by weathering processes such as the wind, rain, glaciers, wave action and flowing water.

Evaporate: To change from liquid into a gas or vapour.

Extinct: Not existing any more. Species of animals (such as the Dodo) that do not exist any more are said to be extinct.

Fallow: Land that has been left without planting. Leaving farmland fallow allows it to rest. This is a natural way of restoring its fertility.

Fertile: Fruitful, producing good crops. Fertile soil is rich in the nutrients and materials needed by plants for healthy growth.

Fertilizers: Substances which are added to the soil to make it more fertile. Fertilizers can be made from either natural or artificial materials.

Fossil fuels: Fuels made from the remains of plants and animals that lived millions of years ago in the geological past. The main fossil fuels are coal, oil and gas.

Hectare: A unit of area in the metric system equal to 10,000 square metres or nearly $2\frac{1}{2}$ acres.

Humus: A dark, rich organic material that is made from the decomposed remains of dead leaves and plants. Humus is essential to the fertility of the soil.

Hydrosphere: All the waters of the Earth's surface. These include the waters of oceans, lakes and rivers, ground water, the water vapour in the Earth's atmosphere and the frozen water of the polar ice-caps and glaciers.

Inorganic: Not organic or made of living substances.

Irrigation: Supplying land or crops with water by means of streams, canals and pipes. The use of irrigation has made it possible for farmers to grow crops in **arid** regions and other places lacking sufficient rainfall or other natural sources of water.

Krill: The name given to many different types of small shrimp-like animals that live in all oceans.

Loess: A type of fine, light-coloured soil, which is found in many areas of Asia, Europe and North America. Loess is thought to be a thick layer of dust that was deposited by the wind in the Ice Age. In some places it is hundreds of metres thick.

Magma: Molten rock found in the Earth's interior. Sometimes it comes to the surface as lava from volcanoes. When it cools underground it forms igneous rocks.

Marginal: At the edge, existing on the margin or at the limit. Marginal lands are commonly found in the semi-arid regions of the world, often on the edges of deserts.

Mass: The amount of matter in a body.

Meteorites: Meteors are lumps of stone or metal moving rapidly through outer space.

Microbes: Animals that are so small they can be seen only with the aid of a microscope.

Micro-organisms: Organisms that cannot be seen with the naked eye. Bacteria and viruses are two common types of micro-organisms.

Nutrients: Substances which provide nourishment. Food is the main source of nutrients for people. Plants get most of their nutrients from the soil.

Organic: Made of or from living things. Manure and compost are organic fertilizers. Fossil fuels are organic fuels made from the remains of plants.

Pesticides: Poisonous substances which kill animal or insect pests. The build-up of pesticides in the environment is an increasingly worrying ecological problem.

Photosynthesis: The process by which green plants make their food. Plants use the Sun's energy to turn carbon dioxide from the air and water from the soil into food. While making their food, they give off oxygen and water vapour.

Plankton: Very tiny living marine animals. Some live in the ocean and some live in fresh water. Most are microscopic.

Pollutants: Undesirable or harmful substances that poison the environment. Pesticides, factory effluents, sewage, smoke and nuclear radiation are some of the most common pollutants.

Precipitation: Precipitation is a term for any of the forms of water, liquid or solid, that fall to the ground from clouds.

Predatory: Animals that live by hunting and preying upon other animals.

Preservative: A substance that keeps a thing safe or in good condition.

Radiation: The giving out of rays from an object. Not all radiation is harmful. The Sun and the stars, for example, give out radiation in the form of light and heat.

Radioactive: Giving out atomic energy.

Resources: Things that can be used. The natural resources of a country are its mineral wealth, its power sources, its land and, most importantly, its people.

Salinization: The process of making land salty. Poorly designed irrigation works can lead to the deposit of salts on the land.

Savannah: A grassy plain in hot regions of the world with few or no trees. There are savannah lands in Africa and South America.

Scrubbers: Devices that capture harmful pollutants and make them harmless. Some scrubbers are attached to chimneys to stop harmful gases from escaping into the atmosphere.

Solar storms: Brief, but powerful, bursts of solar radiation. These bursts of radiation are caused by sun-spots, periods of intense activity on the Sun's surface.

Solar system: The Sun and the heavenly bodies (planets – including the Earth – and their moons and asteroids) which move around it.

Species: A group of animals or plants which are alike physically and genetically.

Steppe: A dry, grassy plain with few trees and located in cold regions of the globe.

Toxic: Something that is poisonous.

Trace elements: Elements naturally present in very tiny amounts. Trace elements in soil are vital for healthy plant growth.

Transpiration: The giving off of water vapour through the leaves of plants.

Tropics: Hot areas of the Earth. The Tropics are two imaginary lines drawn around the globe. The Tropic of Cancer is about 23° north of the Equator. The Tropic of Capricorn is about 23° south of the Equator.

Tundra: Vast level treeless plains of the Arctic regions of the Soviet Union and Canada. Tundra differs from **steppe** in that its subsoil is frozen all year round.

Weathering: To wear away as a result of the action of wind, rain, sun, and waves.

Windbreaks: A screen or row of trees or fencing that shields and protects something from the full force of the wind. Windbreaks are extremely useful ways of combating wind **erosion** and are frequently parts of **afforestation** projects.

Zone: A region, district or area that has particular features, characteristics or properties.

Index

A **Bold** number shows the entry is illustrated on that page. The same page often has writing about the entry too.